AF553287

LISE

Library and Information Science Education (LISE)

Based on UGC-CBCS Guideline

L I S E

Library and Information Science Education (LISE)

Based on UGC-CBCS Guideline

PRAVAKAR RATH

LISE: Library and Information Science Education (LISE)
Based on UGC-CBCS Guideline
Pravakar Rath

First Published 2016

ISBN 978-93-5002-397-6

Published by
AAKAR BOOKS
28 E Pocket IV, Mayur Vihar Phase I, Delhi 110 091
Phones: 011 2279 5505, 2279 5641
aakarbooks@gmail.com

Printed at
Saurabh Printers Pvt. Ltd., Greater Noida

Contents

Preface

Quality of library and information services reflects the quality of professional manpower available in the country. In other words, the quality of library and information science education determines to a large extent the quality of library and information services available to the customers. Therefore, library education must be given the greatest attention that it deserves. Library and Information Science Education is at the crossroads. There is an absolute need of the LIS education which need to be revamped, redesigned, using innovation to meet the information needs of knowledge based society. In the present day technology driven society, Library educators must accept this challenge and respond adequately. There is a need for innovation and redesigning the courses to meet the challenges. Library schools should serve as laboratories, experimenting with new courses, teaching methodologies, tools, new environment. The field of library and information science education is a dynamic one. Rapid changes are taking place in terms of curriculum, admission procedures, teaching methods and techniques, examination and evaluation in recent years. It has been greatly affected by application of Information and Communication technology (ICT). It is a tool that has changed the very shape of LIS programme including teaching and learning process.

Internationalization of higher education in general and

Library and Information Science Education (LISE) in particular are constantly facing challenges in order to make it more competitive, creating innovative skills, fulfilling the expectations of the potential employers in job market and finally to make it more student/learner centric. Along with many qualitative measures introduced by the Ministry of Human Resource Development (MHRD) and University Grants Commission (UGC), introduction of Choice Based Credit System (CBCS) both at PG and UG level have been made mandatory for all the universities and colleges under University Grants Commission. Although there are very less number of colleges offering Library Science at UG level, a good number of universities offering PG level Library and Information Science attached to central and state universities. Introduction of Choice Based Credit System has allowed more flexibility, seriousness, mobility, specialization, know your progress through continuous evaluation combining with a number of teaching learning strategies like, Lectures, practical, tutorial, seminar and colloquiums, group discussions, presentation, tests and assignments, field visits, projects and dissertations. All these activities have developed the seriousness of the learners which have a great impact on his/her academic and professional career. The design of CBSC curriculum and syllabus, credit distribution to each course, minimum qualifying marks for up gradation to the next semester, selection of Open Elective course by each student, tabulation of all the four semester marks for final Gradation and award of Degree are unique in nature and maintains full transparencies among the students, departments and university level as well.

The present publication entitled: *LISE: Library and Information Science Education based on UGC-CBCS Guideline* is an outcome of the experience gained while associated with different universities and UGC including Mizoram university. As an innovative and dynamic step introduced by UGC in the best interest of the students, many universities are in the process of introducing the same or already introduced. The most difficult task faced by the departments to select the appropriate courses and its contents (FC, CC, SC, OE) which have great relevance in the present context and more importantly relevant to the job market as a professional course. Besides distribution of credit to each course as per UGC guideline is another challenge for LIS educators. All these reasons prompted me to bring out this publication which will serve as a model to many PG teaching departments in India whether already introduced or in the process or planning to introduce.

I take this opportunity to express my sincere thanks to all my colleagues in Mizoram University for contributing their academic inputs while designing latest MLIS Syllabus based on UGC-CBCS model (2015) besides my own experience gained in various universities and national level institutions at PG, M.Phil and Doctoral level.

I would like to express my heartfelt gratitude for getting full encouragement and inspiration from my wife Dr Moorttimatee Rath and daughter Manasa Rath to contribute something to the profession in the form of publication.

I am also thankful to Aakar Books for accepting my request to bring out this publication.

Pravakar Rath

1

Library and Information Science Education in India: Issues and Concerns

"Librarianship" over the period of time has become an established discipline of study and changed over to Library Science, Library and Information Science, Information Studies in India. Many of the developed countries including USA and Canada have named it Library and Information Studies or Information and Library Studies or Communication, Information and Library Studies. Some of the universities in Canada and Australia are offering only "Information Studies" despite the fact that these courses are originated from Library Science. Besides, growth and development of new information society, knowledge society, advances in information and communication technologies and its impact on library and information workplaces have necessitated reorienting the existing library professionals into information professionals. Information professionals are expected to strategically use information in his/her job to advance the mission of the organization and accomplish this through the development, deployment and management of information sources and services. The schools of library and information studies in general and LIS educators in particular play an important role in design, development and delivery of library and information science programmes by providing appropriate education and training in creating appropriate human resources befitting to the changing information scenario,national and global job market.

The author having served for more than thirty one years in the capacity of a Librarian and academician understands the ground realities and problems faced by the LIS education in India. There are resources problems like physical, human and financial faced by the Departments/Universities/State Governments. Although central universities are comparatively in a better position than state universities, education in Librarianship should maintain national and international standards. UGC also emphasizes internationalization of education so that our products are in compatible with international standards. All these problems and issues need to be addressed and it is high time to revamp and suggest measures to be undertaken by the universities/Sate and Central government to evolve appropriate policies, standards and guidelines for quality education in library and information science.

The author of the present publication was awarded with a Major Research Project by UGC in 2007 and conducted a survey of Library and Information Science schools in India and solicited their suggestions for qualitative development of LIS education keeping in view the global developments, job market and expected level of competency development of the learners. As on date there are more than 95 schools of library and information studies attached to universities as PG Departments. Out of these, 45 schools responded to my questionnaire and their suggestions were analyzed and presented for qualitative development of LIS education in India. Besides there are a good number of open universities and Correspondence Course Institutes attached to universities and institutions offering LIS courses through distance mode which did not form the part of the research project.

Quality of LIS education further depends upon on regular interaction and coordination among the LIS educators, practitioners and researchers. Leading experts in LIS education, University Librarians, IIT Librarians, Researchers and other practicing librarians were interviewed and consulted to make the study more pragmatic and innovative keeping in view the global trends with local insight.

LIS Education: Quality Assurance

Accreditation is an effective mechanism for improvement and maintenance of standards in institutions and their programmes. The following reasons stress the need for accreditation of Library and Information Science Education in India:

a) To achieve uniformity and to cater the information needs of the country.
b) Difference in languages and medium of instruction, absence of quality reading materials in the regional languages and mobility of the qualified people at national level.
c) Wide disparity in course contents including the core courses and optional.
d) Absence of revision policy pertaining to course contents.

With the alarming increase in the number of library schools, the qualities of the training programmes have certainly got affected adversely. At present there is no system of accreditation as such of the library schools at the national level. The UGC is entrusted with the responsibility of ensuring and maintaining proper academic standards of higher education in the country but till now its role has generally been of a recommendatory in nature rather than of an accrediting agency. For example, Bar Council of India and Indian Medical Council are the accrediting agencies as far as legal and medical education are concerned. NAAC has mandate of only institutional accreditation.

In USA and Canada, ALA was the first recognized accrediting agency and later the council of National Academic Awards was established. In UK The Library Association is the accrediting agency. A separate national body of accrediting the LIS courses in India is need of the hour.

Impact of ICT on LIS Education-Challenges

The impact of information and communication technology has a direct bearing not only on the library and Information profession but on the LIS education as well. So far the emerging technologies and their applications have not been paid proper attention in imparting practical training to the LIS education. The LIS schools are finding it difficult to design inter-disciplinary curricula for education and training. Unless the professional education adopts the topics on changing technologies and their related techniques like databases, online retrieval, records management archives and marketing of information, it would become obsolete. The professional experts visualize a threat from the computer professionals, systems, analysts, communication specialists, scientists and technocrats who are slowly encroaching upon our profession.

The LIS curriculum is expected to provide trained personnel capable of handling information, managing information and dissemination functions from libraries and information centers more effectively even in a technological environment. To cope with the changing environment there is a need for revising the existing curricula in LIS schools. The curriculum Development Committee (UGC) on Library and Information Science (2002) in its report made several recommendations. The main recommendations include,

1. The LIS courses should improve their quality, in particular by the incorporation of advancing information technology.
2. Paraprofessional training courses may be undertaken by other appropriate agencies but care must be taken to ensure uniformity and quality of such training all over the country.
3. LIS professionals must be given every facility to refresh his/her expertise, so as to keep abreast of advancing knowledge by a planned development of continuing education programmes in the field.
4. There should be an accreditation agency to ensure the standard and quality of the training in LIS field.
5. There is a national need for furthering higher education and research in LIS, which may be undertaken by a National Centre to be established for the purpose.

Professional responses to the "information problem" by LIS have been richly varied along a continuum from the diagnosis of individual user problems and the provision of resources from which potential solution might be derived to the design and implementation of new information systems and organizational schemes. The LIS profession has developed an array of service models and tools to address the "information problem" as it has framed it. In general, these models and tools have been grounded in a knowledge base consisting of an understanding of the following areas:

This knowledge base has been applied in libraries along four dimensions:

- **Tool Making**

  It concerns to developing systems of organization, mechanisms for retrieval of information-bearing objects, and forms of information service. Examples include catalogs, cataloging rules, and classification systems;

- **Information Management**

  Applying the tools used for information storage, organization and retrieval. This dimension forms the context of daily practice for most librarians and includes the application of tools for organization of information and "collections" (e.g., LCSH, LCC, and Dewey);

- **Agency (or Service)**

  Acting as intermediaries (e.g., reference services) or directly as agents on behalf of users, and educating users to better act on their own behalf;

- **Management of Information Organizations**

  Designing, managing, and operating information organizations, organizational units, and systems.

The traditional focus of LIS practice and education on the library as an enterprise and an institution largely remains the controlling factor in defining its arena of professional practice both in the eyes of both the profession's members and the public. This is true despite the broad potential application of its knowledge base in a range of contexts beyond the library (e.g., business and government) a trend in LIS education towards expanding its market to other information functions and organizations, and the decline in library jobs, especially those in the public and quasi-public sectors such as public and university libraries.

At all levels of society, policy makers and common people alike are becoming more aware of what it means to live in the information age. It is clear to many that:

- There will be a rapidly increasing need for information management in all of our organizations;
- Libraries are only one part of the information industry and for many segments of the society they are not the most important part;
- Librarians will become an increasingly smaller proportion of information workers; and
- Problems of information management are, more than ever, interdisciplinary-requiring knowledge and skills from areas that were once seen as peripheral to the heart of our field.

Much of the discussion about this change has focused on technology-driven factors including:

- The fusion of computing and telecommunications, producing a geographically distributed environment for creating, storing, manipulating, and sharing information;
- The fusion of media into a unified stream of bits giving rise to the need for information design for multi- and hypermedia and new ways of interacting and assimilating information;
- Increased abundance and complexity of information through globally accessible networks and multi- and hypermedia information structures; and
- The emergence of what John Seely Brown of Xerox PARC calls social, as opposed to personal, computing in which global networks coupled with advanced computing technologies will facilitate learning communities of geographically-dispersed people and information resources.

Another critical and important environmental change is the increase in the value of information as a strategic commodity. Its acquisition and control are a source of power between and within organizations. The magnitude, scope, and growth of the information economy are well documented. Information activities are becoming more important within organizations of all kinds. Increases in productivity depend on information applied to production, consumption, distribution, and trade, particularly as the complexity or productivity of the economy increases.

Information's role in creating power and wealth is attracting the attention of powerful new players, including other professions such as computer science and business administration. Both the professional and educational components of LIS are facing new competition. The traditional focus of LIS has not been on information at all but rather on its containers — books, journals, maps, images, and so on. It acquires, describes, stores, and disseminates them without much concern for how their intellectual content is used.

The changes brought about by developments in the information environment are double-edged for LIS. New means of information storage, manipulation, retrieval, and dissemination offer opportunities that LIS might well claim as its own. However, these developments threaten major changes in the roles of libraries, the LIS profession, and LIS education as other professions move into this area of professional practice.

LIS Schools in India: Issues and Concerns

LIS education in India has just completed 100 years. Schools of library and information studies and faculty members are constantly facing challenges to improve its quality due to global developments. Some of the issues and concerns that LIS schools are facing today are stated below.

Need for National Accreditation Agency

For quality assurance and maintenance of standards, there is a need for national accreditation agency in India to achieve standards of excellence at national and international level. An accreditation body will ensure adopting best practices by developing norms, standards and guidelines for schools of library and information studies to offer LIS courses at par with national and international standard. This will further allow the LIS degree holders of one country to be accredited by another country. Presently a number of such councils are in operation in other disciplines like Medical Council (legal education), Bar Council (legal education), National Council of Teacher Education (teacher education), and AICTE (technical education). A similar national body namely National Council for Library and Information Science is the need of the hour to maintain standards and assuring quality in library and information science education in India.

Although National Assessment and Accreditation Council (NAAC), an autonomous body inder the University Grants Commission is responsible for institutional accreditation (Universities and Colleges),has recognized the functioning and assessment of "Library" as an essential component and vital sub-unit in assuring quality in higher education. For this purpose NAAC has developed "Guidelines on Quality Indicators in Library and Information Services: Affiliated/Constituent Colleges". But hardly NAAC plays any role in department accreditation.

Internationalization of LIS Education

Changes at work place in a digital/virtual environment have compelled libraryand information professionals to reorient themselves and compete in the global market as well. This has necessitated a radical change in LIS curriculum and syllabus keeping in view the need of information work force required in the international/global market. This will eliminate the wide disparities of LIS education, practice and research between the developing and developed countries. IFLA Education and Training Section is also emphasizing much on issue of equivalence and reciprocal recognition of academic qualifications. The goals of these efforts are to facilitate mobility of students and to increase employability. An emphasis on quality assurance on LIS education internationally cloud give the opportunity for improving the skills of individual students and to increase the quality of national LIS higher education system. Measuring courses in terms of Credits, Credit transfer, Choice Based Credit System are some of the measures to contribute to internationalization of higher education.

Need Based Curriculum

There is a worldwide phenomenon of convergence of library, documentation, information and knowledge areas and a new curriculum design needs to take this fact in to account. An up to date curriculum integrating professional knowledge, skills (managerial, technological and communication) and specializations reflects much on the learners to compete in a national and international potential job market. The appropriate teaching learning pedagogy is planned at this stage to provide and an effective learning environment to the learners.

Competent Faculty

Faculty members play an important role in capacity building (creativity, innovations, transfer of knowledge and capacity to use high technology). Faculty members as innovators could create innovative organizations, competition in the global market and more over the success of the students is considered as testimony of faculty members.

Instructional Technology Support

The technology which can support the effective delivery of LIS courses including new media technology. The present day Information Science discipline incorporates a variety of software requirements to teach Library Automation, Networking and Internet Technology, Multimedia, Digitization, Content Development and other areas of information management. Both print, electronic and web based information resources supplement the teaching curriculum, students, faculty members and researchers. The LIS educators require keeping themselves up to date with latest publications including e-books and e-journals available in the subject. Learning resources through Library Website could provide unlimited access to all categories of users with wide variety and less cost.

Continuing Education Programmes

The schools of library and information studies in general and library educators in particular need to organize continuing education programmes to provide latest developments in the profession and practice in the work place. The programme will provide both exposure and develop professional skills to the participants through refresher courses, orientation programmes, workshops, seminars etc. Rigorous hands on experience aiming at skill/capacity development may be undertaken by the schools of LIS as *"Training to the Trainers"*.

System of Continuous Evaluation

A mechanism of system evaluation has proved to be an accepted parameter to know the strength and weakness of the professional competencies of LIS educators in the changing information scenario. The faculty members could get the feedback from the management to improve their competencies and cope up with emerging areas of specialization. Continuous evaluation of students is equally important through tests, assignments, tutorials, seminars and colloquiums to monitor their progress.

Adequate Financial Support

The quality in imparting higher education and more specifically professional education like library and information science warrants developing appropriate infrastructure/resources (physical, human). Building these resources require adequate financial support to maintain standards of excellence and assure quality in delivering library and information science education.

Schools of library and information studies will continue to face the challenges of digital era. These challenges can be met only when the educators, practitioners and researchers of library and information profession work together and bring qualitative improvement through curriculum which has a great impact on work places. The LIS schools not only to aim at balancing traditional librarianship and technology but to do a lot to make the students exposed and develop expertise on different areas of information and communication technology and its application in library and information centers. The emerging areas of ICT are compelling the library and information schools to revamp LIS education in the country, draw a road map to achieve its mission and prepare a vision for 21st century. UGC in this regard have a very limited role, but many things depend on the individual departments to keep themselves up to date with changing information scenario, understanding the fact that the present national and global job market require a different kind of LIS professionals what it was supposed to be earlier.

Suggestions from Heads of Schools of Studies and Experts

While conducting research project and submitted the final report to UGC in 2010, Heads of the schools of library and information studies and senior experts in the subject suggested a number of measures to be undertaken by the departments, UGC for qualitative improvement of LIS education in India so as to build up its professional image at national and global level.

Curriculum Development

The LIS curriculum designed by the departments need to be a need based curriculum befitting to the national and global job market. Although UGC is responsible to prepare a model curriculum (latest-2002), either this is adopted fully/ partially or not at all. To the extent possible the curriculum should reflect 50:50 ratio of theory and practical components with clear emphasis on Librarianship and ICT components.

A need based curriculum should include library automation, networking and Internet, Information System and Retrieval, Content development, Digital Library, Design and Development of Library Website, Use and Evaluation of Web Resources, Knowledge Management, E-Publishing, Copyright and Intellectual Property Right in electronic environment. A need based and qualitative curriculum can only be designed with the help of Educators, Practitioners and Researchers.

Core and Elective Courses

The curriculum should comprise both the core and elective courses. The core courses should balance the librarianship and technology where as electives or optional papers with wide choice should provide more opportunity of specialization and cater the needs of the industries and specialized organizations in the field of Agriculture, Health, Business and Industry.

Faculty, Teaching and Learning

Faculty is the testimony of success of the students. Trained, specialized faculty with up to date knowledge and skills could deliver teaching and learning more effectively. To achieve the standards of excellence sound professional knowledge, up to date content and good communication skills are the three essential characteristics of a good teacher. The faculty members should be open to self evaluation and accountability.

One of the major targets that we have to achieve is to make our profession more attractive to lure and induct best brains in to it. Teaching and Learning must be laboratory and library oriented. Faculty and student exchange programmes among the leading universities of national and international level shall allow both teachers and students be exposed to latest trends and developments. In the changing information environment, web based education is an added advantage which all the teachers and students should be motivated to access, store and retrieve vast amount of information pertaining to their area of teaching and research.

Physical Resources/Teaching Aids

Physical resources not only include building, furniture and equipment, more important is ICT infrastructure. A well equipped information processing laboratory with computing and network infrastructure including Internet connectivity facilitate practical to be undertaken by the students. Adequate ICT infrastructure need to be developed in each school to supplement teaching and learning activities at regular intervals. Teaching aids include library software, digital library software, LCD, laptop, scanners, printers, etc.

Skills and Competencies

The skills and competencies expected from LIS learners are broadly grouped into following categories.

a) ICT Skills: The changing library profession in to information profession requires ability to handle sophisticated technology including networking and Internet skills.
b) Information Management: The ability to collect, access, store, retrieve and disseminate information to users.
c) Communication Skills: Effective and interactive communication skills of the LIS professionals add value to the library and information centers to cater the potential users. Good communication skills not only make users to understand library services, but an effective means of marketing library and information services.
d) Leadership Skills: The curriculum should also include the ability to develop leadership skills of the LIS professionals to carry forward the plans and policies of the libraries and information centers. in 21st century. To nurture, encourage and reflect intellectual leadership capacity by focusing on student-centered and practice in teaching learning is the need of the hour. Traditional skills of librarianship need to be revamped to suit the digital environment.
    - ***Library Internship/Apprenticeship:*** LIS educators strongly felt the introduction of internship/ apprenticeship as compulsory component MLIS course varying from 3-6 months. This will provide an opportunity to each and every student to expose

themselves various management techniques of a library including ICT application in libraries. Further understanding the practical librarianship, each student can make a choice of his/her career path by developing knowledge and skills in the most emerging areas of LIS profession and demand from the national and global job market.

- ***Learning Resources*:** Inadequacy of both print and electronic resources in the form of latest books, journals, reports, monographs inhibit the academic and research development. Majority of schools of library and information studies in the country are today confronted with financial problem to procure these leaning resources. Peer reviewed national and international journals, research and reference books, guides and manuals and other primary sources of information resources be procured by university libraries to supplement qualitative teaching and learning in LIS courses.
- ***Continuing Education*:** Seminars, conferences, workshops, symposiums refresher courses, specialized training programmes at regular intervals may be conducted. This will provide a platform to educators and learners to expose themselves the latest trend and developments in LIS education and research. Specialized training programmes in collaboration with NISCAIR, NCSI, DRTC, DESIDOC, NASSDOC, INFLIBNET, RRRLF, British Council, American Center could provide opportunity to develop skills in digital library, open source software, institutional repositories, information management, information literacy, etc.

Research

Innovative, original and scientific research in library and information science not only increases the quality of services but solves the practical problems of library and information profession. The emerging areas of research in an electronic and digital environment have posed serious challenges to library and information profession paving a way to entirely transform and meet the challenges. More number of Research Fellowship need to be awarded by UGC, CSIR, DRDO, and ICSSR. Some of the well established LIS departments having required infrastructure and expertise may be recognized as Advance Research Center.

Open and Distance Education

It has been opined by many experts that LIS education through distance mode by open universities and correspondence course institutes are engaged in over production LIS graduates and post graduates and diluting the quality of both the courses and products. There is an immediate need to streamline proliferation of such courses through distance mode. Norms, Standards and Guidelines developed by Distance Education Council should strictly be followed.

Need for a National Accreditation Agency

LIS experts have a serious concern for maintenance of standards or assuring quality in LIS education. Experts have viewed that unlike other national accreditation agencies such as AICET (technical education), NCTE (teacher education), Bar Council of India (legal education) Medical Council of India (medical education), there should be a similar national accreditation body for maintenance of standards in LIS education.

Inclusion of LIS in State/National Public Service Commissions

Some of the experts opined for inclusion of Library and Information Science in state level Public Service Commissions and Union Public Service Commission as well. The profession can be well recognized if it is taught and introduced as an emerging subject at all level.

Looking at the present scenario of LIS education in India, this is still in the developing stage in order to compete with international standard. What is lacking is many universities in India are establishing LIS courses without looking for infrastructure development. These include practical tools, minimum number of teaching staffs, ICT components, library support (books and journals), an uptodate syllabus and continuing education programs for the teachers. The international developments in LIS education and training giving more emphasis on library automation, software applications, networking and internet technology, library website developments, open source software and its application, use and evaluation of electronic information resources, open access initiatives, institutional repositories, intellectual property right, etc. These are the most crucial input for the development of libraries. It provides the necessary strength and resilience to library and information professionals to adequately respond to the changing environment. Therefore, library education must be given the greatest attention that it deserves. Library education in India must evolve along right lines; it must be redesigned innovatively to meet the needs of knowledge based society.

2

Choice Based Credit System in LISE

Globalization has forced the nation to exploit new opportunities including in the areas of higher education which require a proper and proactive policy of internationalization of higher education so as to support the process of creation and distribution of knowledge in Indian universities. This will further help in nation building through application of knowledge and skills to cope with the expectation of 21st century teaching and learning. There is a need for clearer articulation of what is meant by internationalization of higher education. Extending frontiers of knowledge for the larger good of humankind requires that knowledge seekers all over the world join in a common quest for mutual learning. Genuine internationalization of higher education in India would require setting up networks and exchanges of mutual learning with global north as well as global south. India can emerge as an important educational hub for South Asia in particular and also other countries of the developing world. Libraries and information centres play an important role in knowledge organisation and dissemination to supplement the higher education and effective teaching learning process.

Changes at work place in a digital/virtual environment have compelled library and information professionals to reorient themselves and compete in the global market as well. This has necessitated a radical change in LIS curriculum and syllabus keeping in view the need of information work force required in the international/global market. This will eliminate the wide disparities of LIS education, practice and research between the developing and developed countries. IFLA Education and Training Section is also emphasizing much on issue of equivalence and reciprocal recognition of academic qualifications. The goals of these efforts are to facilitate mobility of students and to increase employability. An emphasis on quality assurance on LIS education internationally cloud give the opportunity for improving the skills of individual students and to increase the quality of national LIS higher education system. All these have necessitated the introduction of Choice Based Credit System in the higher education system as part of reforms in higher education by University Grants Commission, a national apex body responsible for planning, policy making and maintenance standards of higher education in India.

Credit and Choice Based Credit System

The credit system followed in higher education is defined as a fixed number of teaching/study hours required for completion of a particular course/programme in a given period or duration. These include class room teaching, tutorial and practical, field study, academic study tour, internship, project/dissertation, seminar and colloquium etc. Reforms in higher education initiated by the Ministry of Human Resource Development (MHRD) and University Grants Commission (UGC), recommendations of National Knowledge Commission in general and Examination Reforms in particular provided for introduction of Semester System, Continuous and Comprehensive Internal Assessment, Choice Based Credit System and mobility of students through effective mechanism of credit transfer across institutions of higher education. It was mandated that the curricula be revised at least once every three years and the syllabi be made relevant in tune with job market dynamics as also in tune with advances in research and development. Institutions were also expected to evolve appropriate pedagogical processes for effective transaction of instructional material.

The Choice Based Credit System allows flexibility of learning and freedom to students to choose courses from other Departments which enable them to bridge the gaps and deficiencies which they may have, in order to meet the requirements of core courses. The introduction of Choice Based Credit System shall enable the students to obtain a degree by accumulating required number of credits prescribed for that degree. The number of credits earned by a student reflects the knowledge and skill acquired by him/her. Each course is assigned with a fixed number of credits based on the contents to be learned. A student has also the choice in selecting course out of those offered by other departments. The credit/grade points earned for each course reflects the student's proficiency in that course .The CBCS enables the students to earn credits across departments and provides flexibility in duration to complete a programme of study. The Choice Based Credit System allows flexibility of learning and freedom to students to choose courses from other departments which enable them to bridge the gaps and deficiencies which they may have, in order to meet the requirements of core courses.

Courses and Components

According to the latest UGC-CBCS guidelines (2015) for the general Master Degree programmes of two years (four semesters) duration like social science and humanities without having practical component shall comprise 80

Credits. The PG programmes with practical components like science courses including library and information science shall comprise 88 credits and professional programmes like MBA carrying 100 credits respectively. There will be four types of courses 1) Fundamental Course 2) Core Course (CC), 3) Specialized/Soft Course (SC) and 4) Open Electives (OE). Fundamental and Core courses are considered as compulsory courses and carry 2 credits and 4-5 credits respectively. Soft courses are designated as more specialized usually of 4 credits each. Open Electives are choice based /interdisciplinary in nature and are selected from within the departments/school or from unrelated disciplines with an objective to seek exposure. Project work/dissertation shall usually carry 8 credits and can go up to 12 credits provided the entire semester is assigned for project work. Project work is considered as a core course with L: T: P pattern as L=0, T=0, P=8. Every credit shall comprise the following components and equivalent contact hours. Further every offered course shall have three components. L-Lecture, T-Tutorial, P-Practical. Lecture comprises class room lecture sessions, Tutorial consists of participatory discussion/desk work/brief seminar presentation. Practical session consists of hands on experience/laboratory experiments/field studies/case studies/project work/dissertation.

One Credit= One hour teaching or two hours laboratory or practical session per week in a semester of 18 weeks. One credit is also equal to two tutorial hours. One credit is equal to one week field training/academic study tour. Up to two credits can be assigned to one month internship.

Adopting CBCS in MLIS–Mizoram University Experience

The department of library and information science was established in 2002 and initially started BLIS one year and MLIS one year duration each which were discontinued and two years integrated MLIS course was introduced from 2005 academic session. The syllabus was further revised and introduced from 2011 academic session. As per the directive of University Grants Commission, all the post graduate departments were asked to adopt Choice Based Credit System. As a result of which the new syllabus as per CBCS guidelines was drafted and got the approval of various statutory bodies of Mizoram University and came in force with effect from August, 2012. The same was further modified and revised as per latest UGC guideline and implemented from 2015 academic session.

Programme Structure: The MLIS course as per CBCS guideline is a practical based course and carries 88 credits and spreading over to four semesters leading to Maser of Library and Information Science (MLIS).Each semester carries courses of 22 credits which include Fundamental, core courses, soft courses and open electives. (FC= 8 Credits; CC=60 Credits; SC=16 Credits, OE=4 Credits; Total 88 Credits) The CBCS guideline further permits open electives in second and third semester. Each semester carries both theory and practical courses of 22 credits depending on the students learning ability as they are newly introduced to the subject of library and information science. The scheme of papers of each semester and their title, type of course (CC, SC, OE), credit distribution of each paper (L: T: P) are explained in the following tables.

FIRST SEMESTER

No	Course Code	Course Name	Credit Distribution L	T	P	Total	Marks
FIRST SEMESTER (Foundation Course=4; Core Courses=18; Total: 22 Credits)							
1	LIS/1/FC/01	Foundation of Librarianship	2	0	0	2	100
2	LIS/1/FC/02	Foundation of Information Science	2	0	0	2	100
3	LIS/1/CC/03	Basics of Information & Communication Technology	4	0	0	4	100
4	LIS/1/CC/04	Organization of Knowledge–Classification Theory	4	0	0	4	100
5	LIS/1/CC/05	Organization of Knowledge–Classification Practice	0	0	3	3	100
6	LIS/1/CC/06	Organization of Knowledge–Cataloguing Theory	4	0	0	4	100
7	LIS/1/CC/07	Organization of Knowledge–Cataloguing Practice	0	0	3	3	100
		Total	**16**	**0**	**6**	**22**	**700**

Note: Foundation Courses should be of 2 credits each. Core Courses (Basic) should be within 2-5 credits each. Soft Courses should be within 3-5 credits each. Open Electives should be of 2 credits each. Core & Specialization Courses may be unitized into 4–6 units as per convenience of the Department. Project work/Seminar/Field work/Internship/Training shall be treated as Core Course.

The First Semester introduces the fresh graduates just admitted in Master of Library and Information Science about fundamental concept of Library and Librarianship. This semester provides the basic understanding and foundation of different kinds of libraries and their functioning, services, national and international organization promoting library and information services. The beginning of the semester also allows students to expose themselves to basics of information and communication technology. Besides, the students are exposed to both theoretical and practical components of organizational of knowledge. The scientific organization of knowledge is mainly divided into classification and cataloguing in which the students are exposed to understand the various classification and cataloguing codes and principles while undertaking the classification and cataloguing of library documents. The department follows DDC 23rd Edition for classification practical and AACR-2R for cataloguing practical respectively.

SECOND SEMESTER

No	*Course Code*	*Course Name*	*Credit Distribution* L	T	P	Total	*Marks*
SECOND SEMESTER (Foundation Course=4; Core Courses=16; Open Electives=2; Total: 22 Credits)							
8	LIS/2/FC/08	Introduction to Information Sources	2	0	0	2	100
9	LIS/2/FC/09	Introduction to Information Sources	2	0	0	2	100
10	LIS/2/CC/10	Management of Library & Information Centres	4	1	0	5	100
11	LIS/2/CC/11	Personality Development & Communication Skill	4	0	0	4	100
12	LIS/2/CC/12	Information Sources & Services – Practice	0	0	4	4	100
13	LIS/2/CC/13	ICT Practical	0	0	3	3	100
14	LIS/2/OE/14	E-Resources	2	0	0	2	100
		Total	**16**	**1**	**7**	**22**	**700**

Note: Foundation Courses should be of 2 credits each. Core Courses (Basic) should be within 2-5 credits each. Soft Courses should be within 3-5 credits each. Open Electives should be of 2 credits each. Core & Specialization Courses may be unitized into 4–6 units as per convenience of the Department. Project work/Seminar/Field work/Internship/Training shall be treated as Core Course.

As and when the semester advances, the second semester further introduces two fundamental courses on information sources and services which appraise the students about different reference tools and their evaluation, types of services like bibliography, CAS, SDI, and documentation. Besides, this semester enables the students to understand the management of Library and Information Centres comprising different management techniques for smooth functioning of the libraries. The other papers include basics of information and communication technology dealing with hardware and software, library automation, networking and digitization, library and information networks etc. There are other core courses namely Personality Development and Communication Skill, ICT Practical, Information Sources and Services Practical. The semester also provides opportunity for the students outside the department to opt for one open elective on E-resources of two credits.

THIRD SEMESTER

No	*Course Code*	*Course Name*	*Credit Distribution* L	T	P	Total	*Marks*
THIRD SEMESTER (Core Courses=12; Specialization/Soft Courses=8; Open Electives=2. Total=22 Credits)							
15	LIS/3/CC/15	Information Retrieval	4	0	0	4	100
16	LIS/3/CC/16	ICT Applications in Libraries – Theory	3	0	0	3	100
17	LIS/3/CC/17	ICT Applications in Libraries – Practice	0	0	3	3	100
18	LIS/3/CC/18	Curriculum Stipulated Study Tour – Tour Report	0	0	2	2	100
19	LIS/3/SC/19A	Academic Library System	4	0	0	4	100
	LIS/3/SC/19B	Public Library System					
20	LIS/3/CC/20A	Preservation & Conservation of Library Materials	4	0	0	4	100
	LIS/3/CC/20B	Information Resource Development					
21	LIS/3/OE/21	Community Information Service	2	0	0	2	100
		Total	**17**	**0**	**5**	**22**	**700**

Note: Foundation Courses should be of 2 credits each. Core Courses (Basic) should be within 2-5 credits each. Specialization Courses should be within 3-5 credits each. Open Electives should be of 2 credits each. Core & Specialization Courses may be unitized into 4–6 units as per convenience of the Department. Project work/Seminar/Field work/Internship/Training shall be treated as Core Course.

After discussing ICT fundamentals in the first semester and practical in second semester, the third semester allows the students to understand its applications in libraries through hands-on experiences to gain both knowledge and skills in the areas of library automation software and digital library software ether available in licensed source or an open source. The semester also allows four soft courses namely, Academic Library System, Public Library System, Preservation and Conservation of Library Materials, Information Resource Development out of which students have to select any two. Besides, there is one open elective for the outside department students namely, community information service. The Curriculum Stipulated Study Tour (CSST) provides opportunity to the students to expose themselves the latest trends and developments in the advanced libraries located in the metropolitan cities of India. The students are supposed to submit a Tour report as an evaluational component for examination purpose and thus considered as a core course.

FOURTH SEMESTER

No	*Course Code*	*Course Name*	*Credit Distribution* L	T	P	Total	*Marks*
FOURTH SEMESTER (Core Courses=14; Specialization/Soft Courses=8. Total=22 Credits)							
22	LIS/4/CC/22	Information Systems & Networks	4	0	0	4	100
23	LIS/4/CC/23	Research Methodology	4	0	0	4	100
24	LIS/4/CC/24	Content Management & Digital Library- Theory	2	0	0	2	100
25	LIS/4/CC/25	Content Management & Digital Library- Practice	0	0	2	2	100
26	LIS/4/CC/26	Job Diary (Library Practical Work)	0	0	2	2	100
27	LIS/4/SC/27A	Intellectual Property Rights & Copyright	4	0	0	4	100
	LIS/4/SC/27B	Knowledge Management					
28	LIS/4/SC/28A	Internet & Its Applications	4	0	0	4	100
	LIS/4/SC/28B	Information Literacy					
		Total	**18**	**0**	**4**	**22**	**700**

Note: Foundation Courses should be of 2 credits each. Core Courses (Basic) should be within 2-5 credits each. Specialization Courses should be within 3-5 credits each. Open Electives should be of 2 credits each. Core & Specialization

Courses may be unitized into 4–6 units as per convenience of the Department. Project work/Seminar/Field work/Internship/Training shall be treated as Core Course.

The fourth and the last semester of two years integrated Master's Degree programmes in library and information science provides opportunity to the student to understand different specialized and technical papers both in theory and practice namely, information systems and network, research methodology, content management and digital library (theory and practice), Job Diary. In research methodology, the post graduate students understand the importance of research, selection of topic, methods and techniques of data collection, analysis, and interpretation followed by report writing. The content management and digital library enables the students to developed both theoretical knowledge and practical skills so as to design and develop library website, content development and management, OCR technology, which are very much needed for job market. The job diary as a core course further allows the students to work for a full semester in the university central library in order to gain practical experiences with regard to library operations and management of different sections and divisions. There are four soft courses offered in this semester out of which students have to opt for two courses only.

The Table below indicates Open Electives Opted by Students in Third Semester (August-December, 2015) as per 2012 CBSC Syllabus

Course Code	*Course Title*	*No. of Students opted*	
LIS/3/OE/18	Intellectual Property Right	Psychology (04), Mizo (05) Mass. Com. (08), Pol. Sc. (01), English (01), Physics (01), Management (07), HAMP (01) Commerce (02)	Total 30
LIS/3/OE/17	Community Information Service	Mass. Com (13), Pol. Sc. (03) Psychology (08), English (01), Management (06)	31

From the very beginning of the semester, each department of the university makes an announcement through circulation of the notice or website the number of open electives offered by concerned department. The students make a choice of two electives to be opted by them and get admitted to that with an application to Head of the department. Now this process is being streamlined by a separate committee giving preference to each student for the open electives opted by him/her. The above table shows the number of students opted open electives offered by Library and Information Science department.

Effective Implementation and Monitoring

This was a great challenge in the initial stage of implementation of the choice based credit system particularly selection of soft courses and open electives. The students were very much confused in understanding the system and proper counseling was very much needed. As per the CBCS guideline each department has to notify their CBCS counselor/mentor and notify the list of open electives offered by each department. The students will make a choice out of these courses and apply for admission in to the interested course. The students need to know the credit pattern of each course, system of continuous assessment and evaluation, earning of credits and award of grades, up gradation to the next semester in case of securing less pass percentage etc. Therefore effective counselling is very much required for the students to understand the whole concept of choice based credit system. Once implemented, regular monitoring is required to remove anomalies and set a well defined procedure in order to guide the students and teachers for its effective teaching and learning outcome. Reforms in higher education in general and internationalization of higher education in particular are the priorities of twelfth five year plan (2012-2017) of University grants Commission in India. Universities and other institutions of higher education are ready to face the challenges of knowledge based economy as the world is becoming more and more interconnected and global markets for skills and innovations. Schools and departments offering various post graduate and doctoral programmes have to revamp their curricula and syllabus to make it more student centric rather than teacher centric keeping in view the demand from national and global job market. Expansion, inclusion and excellence are the main priorities of the higher education authorities in India. In order to bring quality and excellence, it is essential to go for radical academic reforms at par with international standards. Introduction of choice based credit system is one of the major reforms in higher education which has compelled the universities in India to provide more choice based courses and flexibilities in selecting them by the students. Schools of library and information studies in India need to standardise their course to make it more relevant in the changing social needs of knowledge based economy. National level professional forums need to persuade the central government to establish an accreditation agency to ensure quality and maintain standards in library and information science education at Master's level. International professional forums in library and information science can take initiatives to standardise the education in library and information science to widen its scope and coverage for mutual recognition and accreditation.

MZU COURSE STRUCTURE FOR MLIS UNDER UGC-CBCS, 2015

No	*Course Code*	*Course Name*	*Credit Distribution* L	T	P	Total	*Marks*
FIRST SEMESTER *(Foundation Course=4; Core Courses=18; Total: 22 Credits)*							
1	LIS/1/FC/01	Foundation of Librarianship	2	0	0	2	100
2	LIS/1/FC/02	Foundation of Information Science	2	0	0	2	100
3	LIS/1/CC/03	Basics of Information & Communication Technology	4	0	0	4	100
4	LIS/1/CC/04	Organization of Knowledge–Classification Theory	4	0	0	4	100
5	LIS/1/CC/05	Organization of Knowledge–Classification Practice	0	0	3	3	100
6	LIS/1/CC/06	Organization of Knowledge–Cataloguing Theory	4	0	0	4	100
7	LIS/1/CC/07	Organization of Knowledge–Cataloguing Practice	0	0	3	3	100
		Total	16	0	6	22	700
SECOND SEMESTER *(Foundation Course=4; Core Courses=16; Open Electives=2; Total: 22 Credits)*							
8	LIS/2/FC/8	Introduction to Information Sources	2	0	0	2	100
9	LIS/2/FC/9	Introduction to Information Services	2	0	0	2	100
10	LIS/2/CC/10	Management of Library & Information Centres	4	1	0	5	100
11	LIS/2/CC/11	Personality Development & Communication Skill	4	0	0	4	100
12	LIS/2/CC/12	Information Sources & Services – Practice	0	0	4	4	100
13	LIS/2/CC/13	ICT Practical	0	0	3	3	100
14	LIS/2/OE/14	E-Resources	2	0	0	2	100
		Total	14	1	7	22	700

THIRD SEMESTER *(Core Courses=12; Specialization Courses=8; Open Electives=2. Total=22 Credits)*

15 LIS/3/CC/15	Information Retrieval	4	0	0	4	100
16 LIS/3/CC/16	ICT Applications in Libraries–Theory	3	0	0	3	100
17 LIS/3/CC/17	ICT Applications in Libraries–Practice	0	0	3	3	100
18 LIS/3/CC/18	Curriculum Stipulated Study Tour – Tour Report	0	0	2	2	100
19 LIS/3/SC/19A	Academic Library System	4	0	0	4	100
LIS/3/SC/19B	Public Library System					
20 LIS/3/SC/20A	Preservation & Conservation of Library Materials	4	0	0	4	100
LIS/3/SC/20B	Information Resource Development					
21 LIS/3/OE/21	Community Information Service	2	0	0	2	100
	Total	17	0	5	22	700

FOURTH SEMESTER *(Core Courses=14; Specialization Courses=8. Total=22 Credits)*

22 LIS/4/CC/22	Information Systems & Networks	4	0	0	4	100
23 LIS/4/CC/23	Research Methodology	4	0	0	4	100
24 LIS/4/CC/24	Content Management & Digital Library- Theory	2	0	0	2	100
25 LIS/4/CC/25	Content Management & Digital Library- Practice	0	0	2	2	100
26 LIS/4/CC/26	Job Diary (Library Practical Work)	0	0	2	2	100
27 LIS/4/SC/27A	Intellectual Property Rights & Copyright	4	0	0	4	100
LIS/4/SC/27B	Knowledge Management					
28 LIS/4/SC/28A	Internet & Its Applications	4	0	0	4	100
LIS/4/SC/28B	Information Literacy					
	Total	18	0	4	22	700
	GRAND TOTAL	65	1	22	88	2800

(FC= 8 Credits; CC=60 Credits; SC=16 Credits, OE=4 Credits; Total 88 Credits)

3

Foundation Courses

FOUNDATION OF LIBRARIANSHIP

Objectives: After going through the course, the students will be able to:

- understand the concept of library and its role in socio, educational and cultural development,
- acquaint with different types of libraries, library extension services, library legislation, and
- appreciate the role of library associations and institutions at national and international level including professional ethics in librarianship

Unit 1: Libraries—Concepts, Types, Their Role and Development

- Types of Libraries: Features and Functions, Five Laws of Library Science
- Growth & Development of Libraries in UK, USA and India
- Library Extension Services
- Library Legislation, Press and Registration of Books Act, Delivery of Books and Newspapers Act

Unit 2: Professional Associations and Organizations

- Professional Ethics in Librarianship
- Professional Associations: IFLA, ILA, IASLIC, SLA

– Information and Documentation Organizations: UNESCO, NISCAIR, DESIDOC, NASSDOC

Note: This course comprises 2 credits (2L+0T+0P) with internal marks (C1+C2) 40 and semester marks 60 (C3).

RECOMMENDED BOOKS

1. American Library Association. *Information Policies: A Compilation of Position Statements, Principles, Statutes, and Other Pertinent Statements*. Chicago: ALA, 2002.
2. Singh, Sewa, A. Amuddhavalli, and Jasmer Singh. *Challenges and Changes in Librarianship: Papers in Honour of Professor Sewa Singh*. Delhi: B.R. Pub., 2010.
3. Baker, David. *Libraries and Society: Role, Social Responsibility, and Future Challenges*. Chandos Publishing (Oxford), 2011.
4. Khan, Riyazuddin. *Introduction to Library Science*. New Delhi: SBS Publishers, 2006.
5. Khanna, J.K. *Library and Society*. New Delhi: Ess Ess, 2003.
6. Kumar, P.S.G. *Foundations of Library and Information Science*. Delhi: B.R. Pub., 2003.
7. Kumar, S. and Leena Sah. *Public Library Act in India*. New Delhi: Ess Ess, 2000.
8. Esperanza, M. and P.N. Kaula. *Perspective of Library Movement in India: An Account of Various Facets and Phases of Indian Library Movement and the Work and Contribution of Prof. P.N. Kaula, A Tribute on His 71st Birthday*. Delhi: B.R. Pub., 1994.
9. Ngurtinkhuma, R.K. *Public Library in India: Impact on Socio-cultural and Educational Development of Mizoram*. New Delhi: Today & Tomorrow's Printers and Publishers, 2011.
10. Ranganathan, S.R. *The Five Laws of Library Science*. Bangalore: Sarada Ranganathan Endowment for Library Science, 1988.

11. Rubin, Richard E. *Foundations of Library and Information Science*. New York: Neal-Schuman Pub., 2010.

FOUNDATION OF INFORMATION SCIENCE

Objectives: After studying the course, the students shall be able to:

- understand the differentiate the conceptual difference among data, information, knowledge along with intrinsic relationship between information and communication,
- visualize the importance of information society and National Information Policy,
- acquaint with different types of information users and their information needs along with information seeking behaviour models, user education/user study and importance of digital literacy.

Unit 1: Information and Communication

- Data, Information and Knowledge: Conceptual Difference
- Information Transfer Cycle, Information as Resource
- Communication: Channels, Media, Models and Barriers
- Information Society and National Information Policy

Unit 2: Library and Information Users'

- Information Users': Types and Characteristics
- Information Needs, Information Seeking Behaviour Models
- User Education & User Study
- Electronic/Digital Literacy

Note: This course comprises 2 credits (2L+0T+0P) with internal marks (C1+C2) 40 and semester marks 60 (C3).

RECOMMENDED BOOKS

1. Feather, John. *The Information Society: A Study of Continuity and Change*. 4th ed. London: Facet Publishing, 2004.
2. Kumar, P.S.G. *Fundamental of Information Science*. New Delhi: S. Chand & Co., 1999.
3. Kumar, P.S.G. *Foundations of Library and Information Science*. Delhi: B.R. Pub., 2003.
4. McBride, P.K. *Career Award Information and Communications Technology: Foundation Level*. Cambridge University Press, 2003.
5. Prasher, R.G. *Information and Its Communications*. New Delhi: Medallions Press, 2004.
6. Rai, A.N. *Communication in Digital Age*. New Delhi: Author Press, 2000.
7. Rubin, Richard. *Foundations of Library and Information Science*. New York: Neal-Schuman Publishers, 2004.
8. Sharma, C.R. and U.N. Singh. *Information Technology*. New Delhi: Shree Publishers & Distributors, 2003.

INTRODUCTION TO INFORMATION SOURCES

Objective: After studying this course the students shall be able to:

- acquaint with different types of information sources (both print and electronic) with their specific features and characteristics,
- distinguish between general information sources and reference sources along with their evaluation.

Unit 1: Information Sources

- Documentary and Non-Documentary Sources (Human & Institutional)
- Reference Sources: Categories, Characteristics and

Usefulness
- Evaluation of Reference Sources: Print and Electronic

Unit 2: Electronic Sources of Information

- e-Documents, OPAC, Web-OPAC
- Subject Gateways/Portals, Bibliographical Sources, Full text Databases, Bulletin Boards, Discussion Groups/Forums
- Open Access Resources, List Serves, Social Networking Sites

Note: This course comprises 2 credits (2L+0T+0P) with internal marks (C1+C2) 40 and semester marks 60 (C3).

RECOMMENDED BOOKS

1. Chowdhury, G.G. *Information Sources and Searching on the World Wide Web*. London: Library Association, 2001.
2. Chowdhury, G.G. and Sudatta Chowdhury. *Searching CD-ROM and Online Information Sources*. London: Library Association, 2001.
3. Ghenney, F.N. *Fundamentals of Reference Sources*. New York: McGraw Hill, 1980.
4. Higgens, C., ed. *Printed Reference Materials*. Library Association, 1980.
5. Mahapatra, M. *Access to Electronic Information: Papers Presented at the SIS-97, 16th Annual Convention and Conference, 29-31 January, 1997, Bhubebaneswar, India*. Bhubaneswar, Orissa, India: Society for Information Science, Bhubaneswar Chapter, 1997.
6. Padhi, Pitambara. *Reference Sources in Modern Indian Languages: A Study on Oriya Language*. Bhubaneswar: Gayatridevi Publications, 1994.
7. Panda, K.C. and J.N. Gautam. *Information Technology on the Cross Road from Abacus to Internet*. Agra: Y.K. Publisher, 1999.

8. Walford, A.J. *Guide to Reference Materials*. London: Library Association, 1966.

INTRODUCTION TO INFORMATION SERVICES

Objective: This course shall make the students understand to:

- know the difference between traditional and electronic information services including Internet based, and
- visualize the importance of social networking and application of Library 2.0 to provide more services to users.

Unit 1: Information Services

- Information Services: Definition, Scope, Need and Functions
- Types of Information Services: Reference Service, Referral Service, Bibliographic Service, Translation Service, Indexing & Abstracting Services, Reprographic Service
- CAS/Alerting Service, SDI, DDS

Unit 2: Internet based Information Services

- Library 2.0: Concepts, Characteristics & Components
- Synchronous Communication & Content Delivery: Instant Messaging, RSS Feeds, Streaming Media, Podcasts, Vodcasts, SMS Enquiry Service
- Collaborative Publishing Tools: Blogs & Wikis
- Collaborative Service Platforms: Social Networks, Tagging, Social Bookmarking

Note: This course comprises 2 credits (2L+0T+0P) with internal marks (C1+C2) 40 and semester marks 60 (C3).

RECOMMENDED BOOKS

1. Guha, B. *Documentation and Information Services*. 2nd ed. Calcutta: World Press, 1999.
2. Kumar, Krishan. *Reference Service*. Ghaziabad: Vikas Publishing House, 1984.
3. Lancaster, Frederick Wilfrid. *Indexing and Abstracting in Theory and Practice*. Champaign, IL: University of Illinois, Graduate School of Library and Information Science, 1998.
4. Panda, K.C., and J.N. Gautam. *Information Technology on the Cross Road from Abacus to Internet*. Agra: Y K Publisher, 1999.
5. Panley, E.P.C. *Technical Paper Writing Today*. Boston: Houghton, 1979.
6. Ranganathan, S.R. *Reference Service*. Bangalore: Sarada Ranganathan Endowment for Library Science, 1991.
7. Seetharama, S. *Information Consolidation and Repackaging: Framework, Methodology, Planning*. New Delhi: Ess Ess Publications, 1997.
8. Walford, A.J. *Guide to Reference Materials*. London: Library Association, 1966.
9. Gupta, Sangita. *Innovative Challenges in Information Services*. New Delhi: Kutub Publications, 2012.

4

Core Courses

BASICS OF INFORMATION AND COMMUNICATION TECHNOLOGY

Objectives: This course shall acquaint the students with:

- basic components of Information and Communication Technology,
- understanding the development information and communication technology including different software and hardware components and devices; and
- different operating systems, programming languages and database management.

Unit 1: Basics of IT

- IT: Definition, Scope & Components (Hardware & Software)
- Generations of Computers
- Storage Devices, Input & Output Devices, Memory

Unit 2: Operating Systems & Programming Languages

- Operating Systems: Types and Functions
- Study of MS-DOS, LINUX and Windows Operating Systems
- Introduction to Programming Languages

Unit 3: Communication Technology

- Tele-communication: Transmission Media, ISDN,

Multiplexing, Switching Technique
- Networking: Topology and Types of Network, Standards & Protocols
- Network Models (OSI), Networking Devices

Unit 4: Database Management System

- Definition, Objectives & Functions
- Types and Elements of DBMS
- Database Structure and Architecture

Note: This course comprises 4 credits (4L+0T+0P) with internal marks (C1+C2) 40 and semester marks 60 (C3).

RECOMMENDED BOOKS

1. Arora, Ashok, and Shifali Bansal. *Computer Fundamentals*. New Delhi: Excel Books, 2000.
2. Basandra, Suresh K. *Computer Today*. New Delhi: Galgotia Publications, 1999.
3. Chandrasekaran, M., S. Govindaraju, A. Abdul Haq and T.R. Narayan. *Elements of Computer Science*. New Delhi: New Age International, 1996.
4. Jain, Madhulika and Satish Jain. *Introduction to Database Management Systems*. New Delhi: BPB Publications, 2007.
5. Kumar, P.S.G. *Information and Communication*. Delhi: B.R. Pub., 2004.
6. Leon, Alexis, and Mathews Leon. *Fundamentals of Database Management Systems*. Chennai: Vijan Nicole, 2006.
7. Matthew, Neil and Richard Stones. *Beginning Linux Programming*. New Delhi: Wiley India., 2008.
8. Prasher, Ram Gopal. *Information and Its Communication*. Ludhiana: Medallion Press, 2003.
9. Vashishth, C.P., B. Ramesh Babu and S. Gopalakrishnan. *Information, Communication, Library,*

and Community Development: Festschrift in Honour of Prof. C.P. Vashishth. Delhi: B.R. Pub., 2004.

10. Sinha, Pradeep Kumar and Priti Sinha. *Computer Fundamentals.* New Delhi: BPB Publications, 2007.
11. Stallings, William. *Computer Networking with Internet Protocols and Technology.* New Delhi: Pearson Education, 2007.
12. Sybex. *LINUX Complete.* New Delhi: BPB Publications, 2007.

ORGANISATION OF KNOWLEDGE – CLASSIFICATION THEORY

Objectives: This course shall acquaint the students to:

- understand the basic concept and philosophies of library classification;
- know the functions of different classification schemes available; and
- make aware of recent trends and developments in the subject and their application.

Unit 1: Knowledge Organization

- Universe of Knowledge/Subjects: Nature and Attributes
- Modes of Formation of Subjects
- Knowledge Classification and Library Classification; Static & Dynamic Theories of Classification

Unit 2: Classification Schemes

- Species of Library Classification Schemes
- Salient Features of DDC, UDC, and CC
- Mapping of Subjects in DDC, UDC and CC

Unit 3: Library Classification Theory

- Definition, Need and Purpose of Classification

- Planes, Canons, Principles, Fundamental Categories, Postulates, Facet Analysis and Facet Sequence
- Phase Relation, Common Isolates, Devices, Mnemonics

Unit 4: Notational Techniques and Recent Trends

- Notation: Definition, Types, Functions, Qualities and Techniques
- Design and Development of Classification Schedules
- Recent Trends in Library Classification

Note: This course comprises 4 credits (4L+0T+0P) with internal marks (C1+C2) 40 and semester marks 60 (C3).

RECOMMENDED BOOKS

1. Broughton, Vanda. *Essential Classification*. London: Facet, 2004.
2. Dhiman, Anil Kumar and Yashoda Rani. *Learn Library Classification*. New Dehli: Ess Ess Publications, 2005.
3. Husain, Shabahat. *Library Classification: Facets and Analysis*. New Delhi: B.R. Pub., 2004.
4. Jennex, Murray E. *Knowledge Management: Concepts, Methodologies, Tools, and Applications*. Hershey, PA: Information Science Reference, 2008.
5. Kao, Mary L. *Cataloguing and Classification for Library Personnel*. Mumbai: Jaico, 2003.
6. Kumar, P.S.G. *Knowledge Organization, Information Processing and Retrieval: Theory*. Delhi: B.R. Pub., 2003.
7. Pathak, Lalit P. *Sociological Terminology and Classification Schemes*. New Delhi: Mittal Publications, 2000.
8. Ranganathan, S.R. *Philosophy of Library Classification*. Bangalore: Ess Ess, 2006.
9. Singh, Sonal. *Universe of Knowledge: Structure &*

Development. Jaipur: Raj Publishing House, 1998.

10. Sood, S.P. *Universe of Knowledge and Universe of Subjects*. Jaipur: G. Star Printers, 1998.
11. Taylor, A.G. *Introduction to Cataloguing and Classification*. 10th ed., New Delhi: Atlantic, 2007.

ORGANISATION OF KNOWLEDGE – CLASSIFICATION PRACTICE

Objectives: This course shall acquaint the students with the practical experience of classification using DDC 23rd edition to classify simple, compound and complex title of interdisciplinary and multidisciplinary in nature.

(A) Assigning Class Numbers representing Simple, Compound, Complex Subjects according to DDC (Latest available edition- 23rd Edition)

(B) Viva Voce

Note: This course comprises 3 credits (0L+0T+3P) with internal marks (C1+C2) 40, Semester marks 50 and Viva-voce 10 = 60 (C3).

RECOMMENDED BOOKS

1. Comaromi, John P., Margaret J. Warren and Melvil Dewey. *Manual on the Use of the Dewey Decimal Classification*. Albany, NY: Forest Press, 1982.
2. Dewey, Melvil, Joan S. Mitchell, Julianne Beall, Rebecca Green, Giles Martin and Michael Panzer. *Dewey Decimal Classification and Relative Index*. Dublin, OH: OCLC Online Computer Library Center, 2011.
3. Dewey, Melvil. *Dewey Decimal Classification and Relative Index*. Edited by Joan S. Mitchell, Julianne Beall, Rebecca Green, Giles Martin and Michael Panzer. 23rd ed. Dublin, OH: OCLC Online Computer Library Center, 2011.
4. Dhyani, Pushpa. *Classifying with Dewey Decimal Classification*. New Delhi: Ess Ess Publications, 2006.

5. Khan, M.T.M. *Dewey Decimal Classification*. New Delhi: Shree, 2005.
6. Mortimer, Mary. *Learn Dewey Decimal Classification (Edition 22)*. Friendswood, TX: Total Recall Pub., 2007.

ORGANISATION OF KNOWLEDGE – CATALOGUING THEORY

Objectives: This course shall acquaint the students with the organization of knowledge with different basic concepts and philosophies of library cataloguing, rules of filing entries and subject headings in cataloguing and understand the different bibliographic standard available and application.

Unit 1: Cataloguing Principles

- Catalogue: Definition, Objectives, Functions
- Types of Catalogue and Physical Forms of Catalogue
- Principles of Cataloguing: Ranganathan's Cannon, Paris Principles
- Introduction to Catalogue Codes: CCC, AACR-IIR

Unit 2: Entry Elements, Filing Rules & Subject Headings

- Kinds of Entries and their Elements of Description
- Elements of Bibliographic Description of Non-Book Material (AACR-IIR)
- Rules for Choice and Rendering of Headings in AACR –IIR
- Subject Heading Lists: Sears List & LCSH

Unit 3: Standards of Bibliographic Description

- ISBD, FRAD (Functional Requirements for Authorized Description), GARR (Guidelines for Authority Records and References), RDA (Resource Description and Access)
- Standards for Bibliographic Information Interchange

and Communication- ISO 2709, Z39.50, Z39.71
- ISBN & ISSN

Unit 4: Bibliographic Record Formats& Other Aspects

- Bibliographic Records Format-MARC 21, UNIMARC, CCF
- Cataloguing of E-Resources- Metadata Standards (Dublin Core)
- Derivatives of Cataloguing (Copy Cataloguing)

Note: This course comprises 4 credits (4L+0T+0P) with internal marks (C1+C2) 40 and semester marks 60 (C3).

RECOMMENDED BOOKS

1. Andrew, Paige G. *Cataloging Sheet Maps: The Basics*. New York: Haworth Information Press, 2003.
2. Aswal, Rajendra Singh. *MARC 21 Cataloging Format for 21st Century*. New Delhi: Ess Ess Pub., 2004.
3. Dhawan, K.S. *Online Cataloguing Systems*. New Delhi: Commonwealth Publishers, 1997.
4. Dhiman, Anil Kumar. *Cataloguing of Non Book Materials*. New Delhi: Ess Ess Publications, 2004.
5. Kumar, Girja and Krishan Kumar. *Theory of Cataloguing*. Delhi: Vikas Pub. House, 2004.
6. Gredley, Ellen and A. Hopkinson. *Exchanging Bibliographic Data: MARC and Other International Formats*. Ottawa: Canadian Library Association, 1990.
7. Hagler, Ronald. *The Bibliographic Record and Information Technology*. Chicago: American Library Association, 1997.
8. Joint Steering Committee. *Anglo-American Cataloging Rules*. Chicago: American Library Association, 2002.
9. Kao, Mary L. *Cataloguing and Classification for Library Personnel*. Mumbai: Jaico, 2003

10. Leigh, Gernert. *A Text Book of Cataloguing*. New Delhi: Dominant Publishers, 2003.
11. Mitchell, Anne M. and Brian E. Surratt. *Cataloging and Organizing Digital Resources: A How-to-do-it Manual for Librarians*. London: Facet Publishing, 2005.
12. Roe, Sandra K. *The Audio Visual Cataloguing*. New York: Haworth Press, 2002.
13. Sharma, Pandey S.K. *Library Cataloguing Theory*. New Delhi: Sahitya Prakashan, 2001.
14. Singh, S.N. and H.N. Prasad. *Cataloguing Manual AACR-II*. Delhi: B.R. Pub., 1985.
15. Sood, S.P. *Theory of Library Cataloguing*. Jaipur: Raj Publishing House, 1999.
16. Taylor, A.G. *Introduction to Cataloguing and Classification*. 10th ed. New Delhi: Atlantic, 2007.
17. Viswanathan, C.G. *Cataloguing Theory and Practice*. New Delhi: Ess Ess, 2008.

ORGANISATION OF KNOWLEDGE – CATALOGUING PRACTICE

Objectives: This course shall acquaint the students with the practical experience of cataloguing like preparation of entries by using AACR IIR and use of subject headings available.

(A) Preparation of Main and Added Entries of Documents according to AACR – IIR (Latest edition) having the following items

- Single Responsibility and Shared Responsibility, Mixed Responsibility
- Corporate Author, Continuing Resources (Serials), Pseudonyms and Anonymous works
- Classics, Non-Book Materials (Cartographic Materials & e-resources)
- Assigning Subject Heading to Documents according to Sears List of Subject Heading (Latest edition)

(B)Viva Voce

Note: This course comprises 3 credits (0L+0T+3P) with internal marks (C1+C2) 40, Semester marks 50 and Viva-voce 10 = 60 (C3).

RECOMMENDED BOOKS

1. American Library Association. *Anglo-American Cataloguing Rules: 2002 Revision: 2005 Update.* Chiacago: American Library Association/CILIP, 2005.
2. Khan, M.T.M. *Anglo-American Cataloguing Rules (AACR).* New Delhi: Shree Publishers & Distributors, 2005.
3. Kumar, Krishan. *An Introduction to Cataloguing Practice.* 3rd ed. New Delhi: Vikas Publishing House, 1986.
4. Ranganathan, S.R. *Classified Catalogue Code: With Additional Rules for Dictionary Catalogue Code.* Bangalore: Sarada Ranganathan Endowment for Library Science, 1988.
5. Satija, M.P. "Sears List of Subject Headings: An Introduction to the Nineteenth Edition (2007)." *Pakistan Journal of Information Management and Libraries* 9, No. 1 (2008): 31-48.
6. Sears, Minnie Earl, Joseph Miller and Susan McCarthy. *Sears List of Subject Headings.* 20th ed. New York: H.W. Wilson, 2010.
7. Singh, S.N. and H.N. Prasad. *Cataloguing Manual AACR-II.* Delhi: B.R. Pub., 1985.

MANAGEMENT OF LIBRARY & INFORMATION CENTRES

Objective: To make the students understand different management techniques, physical, human and financial resources and their application in libraries & information centers.

Unit 1: Management: Concept and Principles

- Principles of Scientific Management in Libraries and Information Centers
- Elements of Management Process (POSDCORB)
- Total Quality Management, Change Management, Disaster Management, Crisis Management, Marketing of Library & Information Services
- Project Management- PERT/CPM, SWOT Analysis, MIS, DSS
- Library Committee- Types and Functions

Unit 2: Physical Resource Management and Library Operations

- Library Building: Site, Selection, Planning
- Furniture, Fittings and Equipments: Standards and Specifications
- System Analysis and Design in Library Operations
- Collection Development and Management – Acquisition, Maintenance, Stock Verification, Weeding out Policy and Procedures
- Preservation and Conservation

Unit 3: Human Resource Management

- Organizational Structure
- Job Description and Analysis: Job – Evaluation
- Inter – Personal Relations
- Recruitment Procedures
- Motivation: Group Dynamics
- Training and Development
- Performance Appraisal

Unit 4: Financial Resource Management

- Resource Mobilization and Outsourcing
- Budgeting, Accounting and Auditing
- Budgetary Control

Note: This course comprises 5 credits (4L+1T+0P) with internal marks (C1+C2) 40 and semester marks 60 (C3).

RECOMMENDED BOOKS

1. Bryson, Jo. *Effective Library and Information Centre Management*. Bombay: Jaico Publishing House, 1996.
2. Beardwell, Ian and Len Holden. *Human Resource Management: A Contemporary Perspectives*. London: Longman, 1996.
3. Chhabra, T.N. *Management and Organisation*. New Delhi: Vikas, 2000.
4. Drucker, Peter Ferdinand. *Management Challenges for the 21st Century*. Oxford: Butterworth-Heinemann, 2002.
5. Evans, Gayle Edward and Patricia Layzell Ward. *Management Basics for Information Professionals*. 2nd ed. New York: Neal-Schuman Publishers, 2007.
6. Johnson, Peggy. *Fundamentals of Collection Development and Management*. 2nd ed. Chicago: American Library Association, 2009.
7. Kotler, Philip. *Marketing Management*. 11th ed., New Delhi: Pearson, 2003.
8. Narayana, G.J. *Library and Information Management*. New Delhi: Prentice-Hall of India, 1991.
9. Paton, Robert A. *Change Management*. New York: Response Books, 2000.
10. Rowley, J.E. *Information Marketing*. Aldershot, Hants, England: Ashgate, 2001.
11. Smith, Judith Read, Mary L. Ginn and Norman Francis Kallaus. *Records Management*. 7th ed. Cincinnati, OH: South-Western, 2010.
12. Stueart, Robert D. and Barbara B. Moran. *Library and Information Center Management*. 7th ed. Westport, CT: Libraries Unlimited, 2007.

13. Stoner, James A.F. *Management: Global Perspectives.* 10th ed. New York: MC Graw Hill, 1996.

PERSONALITY DEVELOPMENT AND COMMUNICATION SKILLS

Objective: To make the students familiarize with personality and communication skills which are essential for a leader to manage the libraries smoothly and successfully. A visionary leader with marketing and public relation capabilities are important characteristics of personality development.

Unit 1: Personality and its Characteristics

- Personality Types, Traits and Characteristics
- Social, Soft and Influencing Skill Development
- Attitude, Appearance, Time and Stress Management Skill

Unit 2: Communication Skill

- Professional Communication Skills (Verbal, Non-Verbal, & Written)
- Communication–Understanding the Audience, Presentation, Body Language, Interpersonal Skills and ability to listening Skill
- Technical Communication Skills and Editorial Tools

Unit 3: Marketing Skills & Public Relations

- Marketing Planning and Strategy
- Publicity and Promotion
- Public Relations and Liasoning with Library Authority and Patrons

Unit 4: Leadership and Vision

- Organizational Ability, Team Leadership and Problem Solving

- Project Management, Annual Plan, Five-Year and Perspective Plan, Disaster Management, Conflict and Crisis Management
- Visionary and Futuristic Approach, Preparation of Vision Document
- Negotiation Skills and Strategies

Note: This course comprises 4 credits (4L+0T+0P) with internal marks (C1+C2) 40 and semester marks 60 (C3).

RECOMMENDED BOOKS

1. Aitchison, Jean. *Teach Yourself Linguistics*. London: Hodder and Stoughton, 1988.
2. Booth, P.F. *Report Writing*. 2nd ed. Kings Ripton: Huntington, 1991.
3. Chandler, Harry E. *Technical Writer's Handbook*. Metals Park, OH: American Society for Metals, 1983.
4. Chandra, A and T.P. Saxena. *Style Manual*. New Delhi: Metropolitan Book Co., 1979.
5. Cooper, Bruce M. *Writing Technical Reports*. New York: Penguin Books, 1986.
6. Gerson, Sharon J. and Steven M. Gerson. *Technical Writing: Process and Product*. Upper Saddle River, NJ: Prentice Hall, 1992.
7. Gladis, Stephen D. *Write Type, Personality Types and Writing Styles*. Amherst, MA: Human Resource Development Press, 1993.
8. Gupta, Sachin. *Personality Development and Communication Skills*. Jaipur, Book Enclave, 2009.
9. Harrison, Colin. *Readability in the Classroom*. Cambridge: Cambridge University Press, 1980.
10. Huckin, T.N. and L.A. Olsen. *Technical Writing and Professional Communication for Non-Native Speakers of English*. 2nd ed. New York: McGraw Hill, 1991.
11. Gray, James G. *Strategies and Skills of Technical*

Presentations. Westfort: Greenwood Press, 1986.
12. Karten, Naomi. *Presentation Skills for Technical Professionals*. Ely: IT Governance Publishing, 2010.
13. Wallace, Harold R. and L. Ann. Masters. *Personal Development for Life and Work*. 10th ed. Australia: South-Western Carnage Learning, 2011.
14. McMurry, Jane Hight. *The Etiquette Advantage: Personal Skills for Social Success*. Wilmington, NC: Stellar Pub., 2002.
15. Sherman, T.A. and S.S. Johnson. *Modern Technical Writing*. 5th ed. Englewood Cliff's: Prentice Hall, 1990.
16. Swain, Dwight V., Joye R. Swain and Dwight V. Swain. *The Issue of Audience. In Scripting for the New Audio-Visual Technologies*. 2nd ed. Boston: Focal Press, 1991.
17. VanAlstyne, Judith S. *Professional and Technical Writing Strategies*. Englewood Cliffs, NJ: Prentice-Hall, 1986.
18. Weisman, Herman M. *Basic Technical Writing*. Columbus, OH: Orenill Publishing, 1980.

INFORMATION SOURCES AND SERVICES – PRACTICE

Objective: To provide students an opportunity to prepare practical records and assignments with regard to providing different types of information services in libraries, information and documentation centers.

Unit 1: Practical Records

The Candidates are required to submit a report on:

- Evaluation of Reference Sources: Print and Electronic
- OPAC/Web OPAC Search Strategy
- Indexing & Abstracting Records
- Current Awareness List
- Bibliography Compilation

Unit 2: Viva-Voce

Note: This course comprises 4 credits (0L+0T+4P) with internal marks (C1+C2) 40, Semester marks 50 and Viva-voce 10 = 60 (C3).

RECOMMENDED BOOKS

1. Choudhury, G.G. *Searching CD-ROM and Online Information Sources*. London: Facet Publishing, 2001.
2. Guha, B. *Documentation and Information Services*. 2nd ed. Calcutta: World Press Private, 1999.
3. Higgens, C., ed. *Printed Reference Materials*. London: Library Association, 1980.
4. Kumar, Krishan. *Reference Service*. New Delhi: Vikas Publishing House, 1984.
5. Lancaster, F. Wilfrid. *Indexing and Abstracting in Theory and Practice*. Champaign, IL: University of Illinois, Graduate School of Library and Information Science, 1998.
6. Ranganathan, S.R. *Reference Service*. Bangalore: Sarada Ranganathan Endowment for Library Science, 1991.
7. Walford, A.J. *Guide to Reference Materials*. London: Library Association, 1966.

INFORMATION AND COMMUNICATION TECHNOLOGY: PRACTICAL

Objective: To provide hands on practice on computer operating systems so as to make the students able to work on Windows and Linux platform for various office works.

Unit 1: Hands on experience of Windows Operating System

Unit 2: Hands on experience of Linux Operating System

Unit 3: Hands on experience of Application Software

- MS-Word
- MS-Excel
- MS-Power Point

Note: This course comprises 4 credits (0L+0T+4P) with internal marks (C1+C2) 40, Semester marks 50 and Viva-voce 10 = 60 (C3).

RECOMMENDED BOOKS

1. Courter, Gini, and Annette Marquis. *Mastering Excel 2002*. New Delhi: BPB Publications, 2005.
2. Cusumano, Michael A. and Richard W. Selby. *Microsoft Secrets*. London: Profile, 2003.
3. Haag, Stephen. *Microsoft Office XP*. Boston: McGraw-Hill, 2002.
4. Jhonson, O. and R. Hanson. *Microsoft Word 2002 Manual for Gregg College Keyboarding & Document Processing*. New York: McGraw-Hill, 2003.
5. Minasi, Mark. *Mastering Windows XP Professional*. New Delhi: BPB Publications, 2001.
6. Norton, Peter, Jill T. Freeze and Wayne S. Freeze. *Peter Norton's Complete Guide to Microsoft Office 2000*. New Delhi: Techmedia, 1999.
7. Perspection, Inc. *Microsoft Word 2002: Simply Visual*. New Delhi: BPB Publications, 2001.
8. Walkenbach, John. *Office 2007 Bible*. New Delhi: Wiley, 2007.
9. Winston, Wayne L. *Microsoft Office Excel 2007: Data Analysis and Business Modeling*. New Delhi: Prentice Hall, 2007.

INFORMATION RETRIEVAL SYSTEMS

Objective: To make the students aware of basics of information retrieval system, indexing systems & vocabulary control techniques and search from database for learning and research.

Unit 1: Basics of Information Retrieval Systems

- Definition, Components and Types of ISAR Systems
- Elements of File Organisation
- Artificial Intelligence and Expert System
- Information Retrieval Models

Unit 2: Subject Representation and Indexing Languages

- Alphabetical Subject Representation
- Contributions of Cutter, Kaiser, Ranganathan, Farradane and Coates
- Characteristics of Indexing Languages
- Vocabulary Control-List of Subject Headings, Thesaurus and Thesaurofacet, Classaurus

Unit 3: Indexing Systems and Techniques

- Assigned Indexing vs Derived Indexing
- Assigned Indexing Systems: Pre-Coordinate (PRECIS, POPSI and Chain Indexing) and Post-Coordinate Indexing System (Uniterm Index System)
- Derived Indexing Systems: Title based (KWIC, KWOC and KWAC), Citation based (SCI, SSCI, etc.) and Full-Text (STAIRS, LEXIS-NEXIS, etc.)
- Automatic Indexing: COMPass

Unit 4: Information Searching and Evaluation

- Search Methods and Search Strategy, Boolean Search
- Information Searching in different Media: Print and Electronic
- Need and Parameters of Evaluation
- Retrieval Performance: Recall and Precision

Note: This course comprises 4 credits (4L+0T+0P) with internal marks (C1+C2) 40 and semester marks 60 (C3).

RECOMMENDED BOOKS

1. Aitchison, Jean, Alan Gilchrist, David Bawden and Jean Aitchison. *Thesaurus Construction and Use: A Practical Manual*. London: Aslib, 1990.
2. Becker, Joseph and Robert Mayo Hayes. *Information Storage and Retrieval: Tools, Elements, Theories*. New York: Wiley, 1963.
3. Chowdhury, G.G. *Introduction to Modern Information Retrieval*. London: Facet, 2010.
4. Convey, John and B. Houghton. *Online Information Retrieval: An Introductory Manual to Principles and Practice*. 4th ed. London: Clive Bingley, 1989.
5. Ellis, David. *Progress and Problems in Information Retrieval*. London: Library Association, 1996.
6. Foskett, A.C. *The Subject Approach to Information*. London: Bingley, 1992.
7. Fugmann, Robert. *Subject Analysis and Indexing: Theoretical Foundation and Practical Advice*. Frankfurt Am Main: Indeks Verlag, 1993.
8. Grolier, Eric De. and Anthony Thompson. *A Study of General Categories Applicable to Classification and Coding in Documentation*. Paris: UNESCO, 1962.
9. Lancaster, F. Wilfrid. *The Measurement and Evaluation of Library Services*. Washington: Information Resources Press, 1977.
10. Losee, Robert M. *Text Retrieval and Filtering: Analytic Models of Performance*. Boston: Kluwer Academic Publishers, 1998.
11. Meadow, Charles T. *Text Information Retrieval Systems*. San Diego, CA: Academic Press, 1992.
12. Sharp, Harold S. *Readings in Information Retrieval*. New York: Scarecrow Press, 1964.
13. Soergel, Dagobert. *Indexing Languages and Thesauri: Construction and Maintenance*. New York: J. Wiley and Sons, 1974.

14. Soergel, Dagobert. *Organizing Information: Principles of Data Base and Retrieval Systems*. Orlando, FL: Academic Press, 1985.

ICT APPLICATION IN LIBRARIES - THEORY

Objective: To keep abreast the students with the automation in libraries, use of advanced version of technology in library operations, aware of the various consortia and consortia-based resources to make them skilled enough to work in an automated library environment.

Unit 1: Library Automation

- Purpose, Planning and Implementation
- Library Automation Software: Types and Features
- Open Source Library Software: Koha, Greenstone and D-Space
- Automation of Housekeeping Operations: Acquisition, Cataloguing, Circulation, Serials Control

Unit 2: Automated Services

- Electronic Reference Services
- Bibliographic and Database Search Services
- CAS/SDI in Automated Environment
- Electronic Document Delivery Service
- Library 2.0

Unit 3: Library Networks and Consortia

- Objectives, scope and characteristics
- Major Library Networks: INFLIBNET, DELNET, OCLC
- Library Consortia: UGC Infonet, INDEST-AICTE, National Knowledge Resource Consortium

Unit 4: Library Security Technology

- Barcode
- RFID
- CCTV, Biometrics, Smartcard

Note: This course comprises 3 credits (3L+0T+0P) with internal marks (C1+C2) 40 and semester marks 60 (C3).

RECOMMENDED BOOKS

1. Chidrupananda. *Making Sense of Library Automation: A Hands-on Guide*. Kolkata: Meteor Books, 2006.
2. Forney, Mathew. *Digital Reference Services*. New Delhi: Dominant Publishers and Distributors, 2003.
3. Gopal, Krishan. *Modern Library Automation*. Delhi: Authors Press, 1999.
4. Grewal, Gagandeep. *Handbook of Library Security*. New Delhi: Dominant Publishers and Distributors, 2004.
5. Rao, N. Laxman. *Library Consortia: Papers: National Seminar on Library Consortia, 22-23 March, 2004, Hyderabad*. Proceedings. Hyderabad: Indian Association of Teachers of Library & Information Science, 2004.
6. Pandey, S.K. *Organisation of Library Automation*. New Delhi: Anmol Publications, 1999.
7. Reddy, Satyanarayana, Shyama Balakrishnan, and P.K. Paliwal. *Automated Management of Library Collections*. New Delhi: Ess Ess Publications, 2001.
8. Siwatch, Ajit Singh and Prem Singh. *Approaches to Modern Librarianship*. Delhi: Sanjay Prakashan, 2006.
9. Sujatha, Gurram. *Resource Sharing and Networking of University Libraries*. New Delhi: Ess Ess Publications, 1999.
10. Tripathi, Aditya, ed. *Open Source Library Solutions: (OSLS)*. New Delhi: Ess Ess Publications, 2010.

ICT APPLICATION IN LIBRARIES – PRACTICE

Objective: To provide hands on experience of library automation software and library website designing tools to make them skilled enough to automate the library as well as design a library website.

Unit 1: Hands-on experience on Library Automation Software

– Integrated Library Software: Koha/SOUL

Unit 2: Hands-on experience on Website Designing

– HTML/Dreamweaver

Unit 3: Viva Voce

Note: This course comprises 3 credits (0L+0T+3P) with internal marks (C1+C2) 40, Semester marks 50 and Viva-voce 10 = 60 (C3).

CURRICULUM STIPULATED STUDY TOUR (CSST) – TOUR REPORT

Objectives: To expose the students an automated and networked libraries on-site, services provided by these libraries and information centers, make a comparative and critical study among these libraries visited and get an overview of latest trends and development on library and information services provided.

(1) Tour Report (70 marks)
(2) Viva Voce (30 marks)

Note: Students are required to prepare a report on working systems and management of selected libraries and information centers of a place outside the state preferably of a metropolitan city. The objectives of this CSST are to:

- acquaint the organization and management of established libraries and information centers at national level;
- expose themselves to automated and networked libraries on-site;

- understand the services provided by these libraries and information centers;
- make a comparative and critical study among these libraries visited; and
- get an overview of latest trends and development on library and information services provided.

Note: This course comprises 2 credits (0L+0T+2P).

INFORMATION SYSTEMS AND NETWORKS

Objective: To make the students aware of the information systems and networks available at national and global level for exchange data and information pertaining to their subject field.

Unit 1: Information Systems

- Definition, Types and Characteristics
- Information Organizations and Systems
- Planning and Designing of Information System
- Evaluation of Information System

Unit 2: National Information Systems

- ENVIS
- BIS
- PIS

Unit 3: Global Information Systems

- AGRIS
- INIS
- INSPEC
- MEDLARS

Unit 4: Networks

- Resource Sharing and Networking – Objectives and Scope
- Features and Characteristics of Library Networks
- Data Networks – NICNET, ERNET, NKN

Note: This course comprises 4 credits (4L+0T+0P) with internal marks (C1+C2) 40 and semester marks 60 (C3).

RECOMMENDED BOOKS

1. Kaul, Hari Krishen. *Library Resources Sharing and Networks*. New Delhi: Virgo Publications, 1999.
2. Lihitkar, Shalini R. *Information Systems and Networks in India*. New Delhi: Today & Tomorrow's Printers and Publishers, 2012.
3. Tedd, Lucy A. and Andrew Large. *Digital Libraries: Principles and Practice in a Global Environment*. Munchen: K.G. Saur, 2005.
4. Neelameghan, A. and K.N. Prasad. *Information Systems, Networks and Services in India.*
5. *Developments and Trends*. Chennai: Ranganathan Centre for Information Studies, 1998.
6. Rowley, J. E. and J. E. Rowley. *The Basics of Information Systems*. London: Library Association, 1996.
7. Shuman, Bruce A. *Issues for Libraries and Information Science in the Internet Age*. Englewood, CO: Libraries Unlimited, 2001.

RESEARCH METHODOLOGY

Objective: To make the students aware of the research methodology concepts, definitions, and various techniques used for data collection, analysis and interpretation in undertaking a research problem independently.

Unit 1: Research and Research Design

- Concept, Meaning, Need and Process of Research
- Types of Research: Fundamental and Applied
- Research Design, Types of Research Design
- Designing Research Proposal
- Literature Search – Print, Non-Print and Electronic Sources

- Literature Review

Unit 2: Research Methods

- Scientific Method
- Historical Method
- Survey and Case Study Method
- Experimental Method

Unit 3: Data Analysis and Interpretation

- Data Collection Techniques: Questionnaire, Interview, Observation, Sampling and Delphi
- Presentation of Data-Tables, Charts and Graphs
- Interpretation of Data: Frequency Distribution, Measures of Central Tendency, Analysis of Time Series, Co-relation Studies and Analysis of Variance
- Use of Statistical Packages

Unit 4: Bibliometric Methods and Report Writing

- Bibiometric Studies: Meaning, Scope and Parameters
- Bibliometric Laws and their Applications
- Informetrics, Scientometrics and Webometrics
- Guidelines for and Preparation of Writing Research Report (Thesis and Dissertation)

Note: This course comprises 4 credits (4L+0T+0P) with internal marks (C1+C2) 40 and semester marks 60 (C3).

RECOMMENDED BOOKS

1. Booth, Wayne C., Gregory G. Colomb and Joseph M. Williams. *The Craft of Research*. Chicago: University of Chicago Press, 2003.
2. Brady, John Joseph. *The Craft of Interviewing*. New York: Vintage, 1997.
3. Gillham, Bill. *The Research Interview*. London: Continuum Press, 2000.

4. Kish, Leslie. *Survey Sampling*. New York: Wiley, 1995.
5. Marshall, Catherine and Gretchen B. Rossman. *Designing Qualitative Research*. Thousand Oaks, CA: Sage, 2006.
6. Nielsen, Jakob. *Designing Web Usability*. Berkeley: New Riders, 2000.
7. Payne, Stanley Le Baron. *The Art of Asking Questions*. Princeton: Princeton University Press, 1951.
8. Raju, Nemani Govinda. *Bibliometric Applications: Study of Literature Use Patterns*. New Delhi: Akansha Pub. House, 2009.
9. Rea, Louis M. and Richard A. Parker. *Designing and Conducting Survey Research: A Comprehensive Guide*. San Francisco: Jossey-Bass Publishers, 2005.
10. Reinard, John C. *Communication Research Statistics*. Thousand Oaks, CA: Sage Publications, 2006.
11. Rowntree, Derek. *Statistics without Tears: A Primer for Non-mathematicians*. London: Penguin Books, 2003.
12. Rubin, Herbert J., and Irene S. Rubin. *Qualitative Interviewing: The Art of Hearing Data*. London: Sage, 2005.
13. Sudman, Seymour. *Applied Sampling*. New York: Academic Press, 1976.
14. Wadsworth, Yoland. *Everyday Evaluation on the Run*. St. Leonards, N.S.W.: Allen and Unwin, 1998.
15. Williams, Frederick and Peter R. Monge. *Reasoning with Statistics: How to Read Quantitative Research*. USA: Harcourt College Publishers, 2001.
16. Willis, Gordon B. *Cognitive Interviewing: A Tool for Improving Questionnaire Design*. Thousand Oaks, CA: Sage Publications, 2005.

CONTENT MANAGEMENT AND DIGITAL LIBRARY – THEORY

Objective: To make the students aware with content management concepts, content developing strategies and digitization of information resources in a library environment.

Unit 1: Content Management & Digitization

- Content Development: Concept; Content Creation & Organization
- E-Content Development Strategies
- Virtual Learning Environment
- Digitization Process, Tools and File Formats

Unit 2: Digital Library Concepts

- Digital Library & Institutional Repository: Concepts; Digital Library Initiatives (National & International)
- Digital Library Software(s)
- Digital Library Creation using D-Space

Note: This course comprises 2 credits (2L+0T+0P) with internal marks (C1+C2) 40 and semester marks 60 (C3).

RECOMMENDED BOOKS

1. Bishop, Ann P., Van House Nancy A. and Barbara Pfeil. Buttenfield, eds. *Digital Library Use: Social Practice in Design and Evaluation*. Delhi: Ane Books, 2005.
2. Chowdhury, G.G. and Sudatta Chowdhury. *Introduction to Digital Libraries*. London: Facet Pub., 2003.
3. Deegan, Marilyn and Simon Tanner. *Digital Preservation*. London: Facet, 2006.
4. Jones, Richard, Theo Andrew and John MacColl. *The Institutional Repository*. Oxford: Chandos Publishing, 2006.

5. Andrews, Judith and Derek G. Law. *Digital Libraries: Policy, Planning, and Practice*. Aldershot, Hants, England: Ashgate, 2004.
6. Lakshmi, Vijay and S.C. Jindal, eds. *Digital Libraries*. Delhi: Isha Books, 2004.
7. Mitchell, Anne M. and Brian E. Surratt. *Cataloging and Organizing Digital Resources: A How-to-do-it Manual for Librarians*. New York: Neal-Schuman Publishers, 2005.
8. Pandey, V.C. *Digital Technologies and Teaching Strategies*. Delhi: Isha Books, 2004.
9. Rajagopalan, A. *Libraries of the Digital Age: Issues & Challenges*. New Delhi: SBS Publishers & Distributors, 2006.
10. Shinde, Ganpati Z. *Emerging Technologies and Future of Libraries Issues and Challenges*. New Delhi: Daya Publishing House, 2015.

CONTENT MANAGEMENT AND DIGITAL LIBRARY – PRACTICE

Objective: To provide students hands on training on content management tools, digital library installation, manage web content development and digital library/institutional repository.

Unit 1: Content Management & Digitization Practice

- Hands on practice of Content Management Software using Joomla
- Hands on practice of Scanner, Digital Camera & OCR

Unit 2: Digital Library Practice

- Hands on practice of Digital Library creation using D-Space/Greenstone
- Creation of Communities & Collection, Submission Process

Unit 3: Viva-Voce

Note: This course comprises 2 credits (0L+0T+2P) with internal marks (C1+C2) 40, Semester marks 50 and Viva-voce 10 = 60 (C3).

JOB DIARY (LIBRARY PRACTICAL WORK)

Objective: To appraise students all the library management functions including acquaintance with library records and their use for which one full semester is allotted for the purpose.

(1) Job Diary (70 marks)

Students are required to prepare Job Diary by working in the University Library or any other library specified by the Department to have hands on experiences in every possible unit/section of a library at a regular basis. The Job Diary is to be submitted by each student at the end of the semester. The diary is to be evaluated jointly by external and internal examiners.

(2)Viva Voce (30 marks)

Note: This course comprises 2 credits (0L+0T+2P). Job Diary/Report carries 70 and Viva-voce 30 marks.

5

Specialized / Soft Courses

ACADEMIC LIBRARY SYSTEM

Objective: To make the students conversant with organization, functions, planning library building, user oriented collections and services in academic library and its role in continuing education program.

Unit 1: Academic Library: Functions and Services

- Role of Academic Library in Higher Education
- Academic Library Services
- Academic Library Management
- Role of UGC for Academic Library Development

Unit 2: Resource Management

- Physical Resources including ICT Infrastructure
- Human Resource Development
- Financial Resource Management

Unit 3: Collection Development

- Collection Development Policy, Weeding out Policy
- Problems in Collection Development
- Role of Library Committee in Collection Development

Unit 4: Staff Development and Continuing Education

- Staffing Norms and Standards
- Continuing Education Program for Academic Libraries

– Personnel Management

Note: This course comprises 4 credits (4L+0T+0P) with internal marks (C1+C2) 40 and semester marks 60 (C3).

RECOMMENDED BOOKS

1. Bose, Kaushik. *Information Networks in India: Problems and Prospects*. New Delhi: Ess Ess, 1991.
2. Cowley, John. *Personnel Management in Libraries*. London: Bingley, 1982.
3. Evans, G. Edward. *Management Techniques for Librarians*. New York: Academic Press, 1983.
4. Gelfand, M.A. *University Libraries for Developing Countries*. Delhi: Universal Books & Stationery, 1974.
5. Kumar, Girja. *Library Development in India*. New Delhi: Vikas Publishing House, 1987.
6. Hingwe, K.S. *Management of University Libraries in India: Principles and Practices*. Calcutta: World Press, 1982.
7. IFLA. *Continuing Education, Issues and Challenges*. New York: Saur, 1985.
8. Issac, Dorothy. *Academic Libraries: Role in the National Development*. Madras: T.R. Publications, 1993.
9. Kent, Allen and Thomas J. Galvin. *The Structure and Governance of Library Networks: Proceedings of the 1978 Conference in Pittsburgh, Pennsylvania*. New York: M. Dekker, 1979.
10. Katz, William A. *Collection Development: The Selection of Materials for Libraries*. New York: Holt, Rinehart and Winston, 1980.
11. Kumar, Krishan. *Library Administration and Management*. New Delhi: Vikas Publishing House, 1987.
12. McDonald, Joseph A. and Lynda Basney Micikas. *Academic Libraries: The Dimensions of Their*

Effectiveness. Westport, CT: Greenwood Press, 1994.
13. McKee, Bob. *Planning Library Services*. London: C. Bingley, 1989.
14. Mittal, R.L. *Library Administration: Theory and Practice*. Delhi: Metropolitan Book Co., 1993.
15. Poole, Herbert and Jerrold Orne. *Academic Libraries by the Year 2000*. New York: R.R. Bowker, 1977.
16. Prasher, Ram Gopal. *Managing University Libraries*. New Delhi: Today & Tomorrow Printers & Publishers, 1991.
17. Ranganathan, S.R. *Library Book Selection*. Bangalore: Sarada Ranganathan Endowment for Library Science, 1989.
18. University Grants Commission. *Report of the Curriculum Development Committee in Library and Information Science*. New Delhi: UGC, 1993.

PUBLIC LIBRARY SYSTEM

Objective: To make the students conversant with organization, functions, building, user oriented collections and services in a public library to serve its purpose as People's University.

Unit 1: Public Library Development

- Public Library: Societal and National Development
- UNESCO Contribution for Public Library Development
- Administration of Public Libraries
- National Agencies for Public Library Development
- Library Legislation

Unit 2: Public Library Services

- Library Services: Types
- Public Library as Knowledge Centers
- Changing Dimensions of Public Library Services

- Evaluation of Public Library Services

Unit 3: Public Library: Resource Development

- Resource Mobilization in Public Library
- Public Library Finance
- Information Resource Development for Public Libraries
- Human Resource Development in Public Libraries

Unit 4: Public Libraries: Trends and Development

- ICT Application in Public Libraries
- Resource Sharing and Networking
- Changing Scenario of Public Libraries in India, UK and USA
- Web based Public Library Services

Note: This course comprises 4 credits (4L+0T+0P) with internal marks (C1+C2) 40 and semester marks 60 (C3).

RECOMMENDED BOOKS

1. *Minimum Standards for Public Library Systems*. Chicago, IL: American Library Association, 1967.
2. Barua, B.P. *National Policy on Library and Information Systems and Services for India: Perspectives and Projections*. Bombay: Popular Prakashan, 1992.
3. Batt, Chris. *Information Technology in Public Libraries*. London: Library Association, 1998.
4. Corbett, Edmund Victor. *Fundamentals of Library Organization and Administration: A Practical Guide*. London: Library Association, 1978.
5. Gardner, Frank M. *Public Library Legislation: A Comparative Study*. Paris: UNESCO, 1971.
6. Gates, Jean Key. *Introduction to Librarianship*. New York: Schuman, 1990.
7. IFLA. *Guidelines for Public Libraries*. Chicago: IFLA, 2000.

8. IFLA. *The Public Library Service: IFLA/UNESCO Guidelines for Development*. Munchen: K.G. Saur, 2001.
9. Iyengar, Sreednidhi, ed. *Library Standards*. New Delhi: Anmol Publications, 1996.
10. Khanna, J.K. *Library and Society*. Kurukshetra: Research Publications, 1987.
11. Kalia, D.R. *Guidelines for Public Library Services and Systems*. Calcutta: RRRLF, 1990.
12. Martin, Lowell A. *Enrichment: A History of the Public Library in the United States in the Twentieth Century*. Lanham, MD: Scarecrow Press, 2003.
13. Murison, W.J. *The Public Library: Its Origins, Purpose and Significance*. London: Bingley, 1988.
14. Patel, Jashu and Krishan Kumar. *Libraries and Librarianship in India*. Westport, CT: Greenwood Press, 2004.
15. Ranganathan, S.R. *Library Administration*. Bombay: SRELS, 1959.
16. Shera, Jesse Hauk. *Foundations of the Public Library; The Origins of the Public Library Movement in New England, 1629-1855*. Chicago: University of Chicago Press, 1949.
17. Venkatòappayya, Velaga, C.P. Vashishth, and P.S. G. Kumar. *Indian Library Legislation*, 2 Vols.: Union Library Bills and Acts. Delhi: Daya Pub. House, 1990.
18. White, Herbert S. *Library Personnel Management*. White Plains, NY: Knowledge Industry Publications, 1985.

PRESERVATION AND CONSERVATION OF LIBRARY MATERIALS

Objective: To make the students appraise need and techniques of preservation and conservation of library materials available in both print and electronic format.

Unit 1: Basics of Preservation and Conservation: Overview

- Preservation and Conservation: Historical Development, Need and Purpose
- Preservation of Print Materials: Books, Periodicals, Pamphlets
- Digital Preservation

Unit 2: Preservation of Non-Print Materials

- Palm Leaves
- Manuscripts
- Films
- Floppies and Disks

Unit 3: Hazards and Control Measures to Library Materials

- Environmental Factor (Temperature, Humidity, Water, Light, Air Pollution, Smoke, Dust, etc.)
- Chemical Factors
- Biological Factors

Unit 4: Binding

- Types of Binding of Library Materials
- Binding Material and their Varieties
- Binding Process
- Standards for Library Binding

Note: This course comprises 4 credits (4L+0T+0P) with internal marks (C1+C2) 40 and semester marks 60 (C3).

RECOMMENDED BOOKS

1. Casey, J.P. *Paper Making*. New York: Interscience Publishers, 1982.
2. Corderoy, John. *Bookbinding for Beginners*. London: Thomas and Hudson, 1978.

3. Dasgupta, Kalpana. *Conservation of Library Materials: Seminar Papers*. Calcutta: National Library, 1988.
4. Dureau, J.M. and D.W.G. Clements. *Principles for the Preservation and Conservation of Library Materials*. The Hague: IFLA Section on Conservation, 1986.
5. Gabriel, M. and D. Ladd. *The Microfilm Revolution in Libraries*. Greenwich: Jai Press, 1980.
6. Harvey, Douglas R. *Preservation in Libraries: A Reader*. London: Bowker Saur, 1993.
7. Hans, K.J. *Sign, Symbol and Script*. London: George Allen & Unwin, 1958.
8. Sharma, Ramagopala. *Panòdòulipi Sampadana Kala*. Dilli: Prabhata Prakashana, 1979.
9. Singh, R.S. *Conservation of Documents in Libraries, Archives and Museums*. New Delhi: Aditya Prakashan, 1993.

INFORMATION RESOURCE DEVELOPMENT

Objective: To acquaint students with various information resource development principles and their selection tools of documents in primary, secondary and tertiary nature.

Unit 1: Types of Information Resources

- Documentary (Primary, Secondary & Tertiary)
- Non-Documentary
- E-Resources

Unit 2: Book Selection Principles

- Drury's Principle
- Dewey's Principle
- McColvin's Principle
- Ranganathan's Principle

Unit 3: Selection Tools

- Current List

- Bibliographies
- Library Catalogue
- Books in Print
- Publishers' Catalogue
- Directories
- WebOPAC (WorldCat)
- Websites

Unit 4: Categories of Documents

- By Physical Characteristics
- By Information Characteristics
- Books and Periodicals
- Theses and Dissertations
- Government Publications
- Grey Literature

Note: This course comprises 4 credits (4L+0T+0P) with internal marks (C1+C2) 40 and semester marks 60 (C3).

RECOMMENDED BOOKS

1. McCloy, Keith R. *Resource Management Information Systems: Process and Practice*. London: Taylor & Francis, 1995.
2. Laudon, Kenneth C. and Jane P. Laudon. *Management Information Systems: Managing the Digital Firm*. New Jersey: Prentice Hall, 2002.
3. Harrell, Margaret C. *Information Systems Technician Rating Stakeholders: Implications for Effective Performance*. Santa Monica, CA: RAND National Defence Research Institute, 2011.
4. McNurlin, Barbara C. and Ralph H. Sprague. *Information Systems Management in Practice*. New Jersey: Pearson, 2003.
5. Okon, E. and Ahiauzu Blessing. *Towards Effective Development of Electronic Information Resources in*

Nigerian University Libraries. Emerald Group Publishing, 2008.

6. Pitschmann, Louis A. *Building Sustainable Collections of Free Third-party Web Resources*. Washington, DC: Digital Library Federation, Council on Library and Information Resources, 2001.
7. Smith, Allen N. and Don B. Medley. *Information Resource Management*. Cincinnati: South-Western Pub., 1987.
8. Rumsey, Abby Smith. *Strategies for Building Digitized Collections*. Washington, DC: Digital Library Federation, Council on Library and Information Resources, 2001.
9. Tariq, Ashraf and Puja Anand Gulati. *Design, Development, and Management of Resources for Digital Library Services*. USA: IGI Global, 2012.
10. Jewell, Timothy D. *Electronic Resource Management: Report of the DLF Resource Management Initiative*. Washington, DC: Digital Library Federation, 2005.
11. Turban, Efraim. *Information Technology for Management: Transforming Organizations in the Digital Economy*. 4th ed. USA: Wiley & Sons, 2008.
12. Smith, William G. *Information Resource Management Policies*. Boston, MA: Database Research Group, 1991.

INTELLECTUAL PROPERTY RIGHTS (IPR)

Objective: To make the students aware of the intellectual property and copyright concepts and other issues related to patents so that students will be aware of IPR and copyright, copyright violation and infringement.

Unit 1: Intellectual Property and Rights

- IP: Concept, Genesis and Development
- Categories of IP

- Enforcement of Intellectual Property Rights and Role of WIPO
- IPR Acts and its Application in Electronic Environment
- Emerging Issues in Intellectual Property

Unit 2: Copyright

- Copyright: Meaning and Scope
- Rights to Copyright Owner
- Licensing of Copyright
- Copyright of Electronic Resources
- Copyright Laws and Related Issues

Unit 3: Patents

- Concept and Scope
- Patent Laws in India and Abroad
- Protection of Inventions

Unit 4: Copyright and Patent Violation and Infringement

- India
- USA
- UK

Note: This course comprises 4 credits (4L+0T+0P) with internal marks (C1+C2) 40 and semester marks 60 (C3).

RECOMMENDED BOOKS

1. Parulekar, Ajit and Sarita D'Souza. *Indian Patents Law: Legal and Business Implications*. Delhi: Macmillan India, 2006.
2. Murray, Andrew. *Information Technology Law: The Law and Society*. Oxford: Oxford University Press, 2010.
3. Wadehra, B.L., *Law Relating to Patents, Trade Marks, Copyright Designs & Geographical Indications*. Delhi:

Universal Law Pub., 2000.

4. Bourgaize, David, Thomas R. Jewell and Rodolfo G. Buiser. *Biotechnology: Demystifying the Concepts*. San Francisco: Benjamin/Cummings, 2000.
5. Correa, Carlos Maria and Abdulqawi Yusuf. *Intellectual Property and International Trade: The TRIPs Agreement*. 2nd ed. London: Kluwer Law International, 2008.
6. Balasubramanian, D., C.F.A. Bryce, K. Dharmalingam, J. Green and K. Jayaraman. *Concepts in Biotechnology*. Hyderabad University Press (Orient Longman), 2002.
7. Bouchoux, Deborah E. *Intellectual Property: The Law of Trademarks, Copyrights, Patents, and Trade Secrets*. Clifton Park, NY: Thomson/Delmar Learning, 2012.
8. Munari, Federico and Raffaele Oriani. *The Economic Valuation of Patents: Methods and Applications*. New Horizons in Intellectual Property Series. Cheltenham, UK: Edward Elgar, 2011.
9. Fishman, Stephen. *The Copyright Handbook: What Every Writer Needs to Know*. Berkeley, CA: Nolo, 2008.
10. Freeman, Lee and A. Graham Peace. *Information Ethics: Privacy and Intellectual Property*. Hershey, PA: Information Science Pub., 2005.
11. Litman, Jessica. *Digital Copyright: Protecting Intellectual Property on the Internet*. Amherst, NY: Prometheus Books, 2001.
12. Grant, John, Charlie Ashworth and Henri Charmasson. *Patents, Registered Designs, Trade Marks & Copyright for Dummies*. Chichester: John Wiley, 2008.
13. Umeh, Jude C. *The World Beyond Digital Rights Management*. Swindon: British Computer Society, 2007.

14. Narayanan, P. *Law of Copyright and Industrial Designs*. Delhi: Eastern Law House, 2010.
15. Cheremisinoff, Paul N., Robert P. Ouellette and R. M. Bartholomew. *Biotechnology: Applications and Research*. Lancaster: Technomic Pub., 1985.
16. Murray, Thomas H. and Maxwell J. Mehlman. *Encyclopedia of Ethical, Legal, and Policy Issues in Biotechnology*. New York: John Wiley & Sons, 2000.
17. Tian, YiJun. *Re-thinking Intellectual Property: The Political Economy of Copyright Protection in the Digital Era*. Routledge Research in Intellectual Property. London: Routledge-Cavendish, 2009.

KNOWLEDGE MANAGEMENT

Objective: To make the students aware of need and concept of knowledge management, its application in libraries and information centers, knowledge management tools and techniques, software associated with and the trends and developments in knowledge management are important features of this course which students will be immensely benefited.

Unit 1: Basics of Knowledge Management

- Concept of Knowledge
- Types of Knowledge
  a) Explicit Knowledge
  b) Implicit Knowledge
- Concept and Scope of Knowledge Management
- Knowledge Management Cycle

Unit 2: Knowledge Management: Creation and Tools

- Knowledge Creation, Access, Transfer and Sharing
- Knowledge Tools
- Knowledge Networks
- Knowledge in Decision Making

Unit 3: Pre-requisites of Knowledge Management

- Sharing of Expertise
- Knowledge Mapping
- Knowledge Worker

Unit 4: Trends and Challenges of Knowledge Management

- KM Initiatives in Indian Organization
- Software for Knowledge Management
- Pioneers in Knowledge Management
- Advances in Knowledge Management

Note: This course comprises 4 credits (4L+0T+0P) with internal marks (C1+C2) 40 and semester marks 60 (C3).

RECOMMENDED BOOKS

1. Anderson, Paul. *Web 2.0 and Beyond: Principles and Technologies*. Boca Raton: CRC Press, 2012.
2. Cappelli, Peter. *The Performance Effects of IT-enabled Knowledge Management Practices*. Cambridge, MA: National Bureau of Economic Research, 2010.
3. Frappaolo, Carl. *Knowledge Management*. Oxford: Capstone Pub., 2006.
4. Atwood, Christee Gabour. *Knowledge Management Basics*. ASTD Training Basics Series. Alexandria, VA: ASTD Press, 2009.
5. Hislop, Donald. *Knowledge Management in Organizations: A Critical Introduction*. Oxford: Oxford University Press, 2009.
6. Awad, Elias M. *Knowledge Management*. 2nd ed. North Garden, V.A.: International Technology Group, 2010.
7. Easterby-Smith, Mark and Marjorie A. Lyles. *Handbook of Organizational Learning and Knowledge Management*. Chichester, West Sussex: Wiley, 2011.

8. Hoffmann, Achim. *Advances in Knowledge Acquisition and Management: Pacific Rim Knowledge Acquisition Workshop, PKAW 2006, Guilin, China, August 7-8, 2006: Revised Selected Papers*. Berlin: Springer, 2006.
9. Becerra-Fernandez, Irma and Rajiv Sabherwal. *Knowledge Management: Systems and Processes*. Armonk, NY: M.E. Sharpe, 2010.
10. Peter, J. Paul and James H. Donnelly. *Marketing Management: Knowledge and Skills*. 10th ed. Boston, MA: McGraw-Hill, 2010.
11. Liebowitz, Jay. *Knowledge Management Handbook: Collaboration and Social Networking*. Boca Raton, FL: CRC Press, 2012.
12. Dalkir, Kimiz, and Jay Liebowitz. *Knowledge Management in Theory and Practice*. Cambridge, Mass.: MIT Press, 2011.

INTERNET AND ITS APPLICATIONS

Objective: To make the students aware of Internet and its related technologies in their day to day use including for academic, learning and research purposes.

Unit 1: Internet: An Overview

- Internet: Introduction, Historical Development and Scope of Internet
- Internet Architecture: H/W and S/W Components, Client/Server Principle, Routers, Connection Types, ISP, Protocols, Uniform Resource Locator, IP Address
- Domain Name System

Unit 2: Web Languages and Web Browsers

- Web: Introduction, History and Functions
- Web Languages: HTML, XML, CSS, ASP, JavaScript, PHP

- Web Browsers: Internet Explorer, Mozilla Firefox, Google Chrome

Unit 3: Intranet and Internet Security

- Intranet: Components, Prerequisites and Services
- Extranet: Components, Prerequisites and Services
- Internet Security: Types of Security, Firewalls, Anti-Virus, Anti-Spyware

Unit 4: Internet Tools and Services

- Communication Tools: Email, Telnet, Discussion Groups
- Search Tools: Gopher, Veronica, Jughead, Archie, Search Engines
- Content Enriching Services: Blogs, Wikis, Social Community Websites

Note: This course comprises 4 credits (4L+0T+0P) with internal marks (C1+C2) 40 and semester marks 60 (C3).

RECOMMENDED BOOKS

1. Bates, Chris. *Web Programming: Building Internet Applications*. 3rd ed. New Delhi,: Wiley-India, 2006.
2. Crumlish, Christian. *The ABCs of the Internet*. New Delhi: BPB Publications, 2007.
3. Hartl, Michael and Aurelius Prochazka. *RailsSpace: Building a Social Networking Website with Ruby on Rails*. Upper Saddle River, NJ: Addison-Wesley, 2008.
4. Kalbach, James. *Designing Web Navigation:*. Sebastopol, CA: O'Reilly, 2007.
5. Miller, Joseph B. *Internet Technologies and Information Services*. Library and Information Science Text Series. Westport, CT: Libraries Unlimited, 2009.
6. Morville, Peter, and Louis Rosenfeld. *Information Architecture for the World Wide Web*. Beijing: O'Reilly, 2002.

7. Morville, Peter and Louis Rosenfeld. *Information Architecture for the World Wide Web.* 3rd ed. Cambridge, MA: O'Reilly, 2006.
8. Nair, R. Raman. *Internet for Information Services.* New Delhi: Ess Ess Publications, 2002.
9. Robbins, Jennifer Niederst. *Learning Web Design: A Beginner's Guide to HTML, CSS, Javascript, and Web Graphics.* 4th ed. Sebastopol, CA: O'Reilly, 2012.
10. Sehgal, R.L. *Intranet and Internet Applications for Librarians.* New Delhi: Ess Ess, 2000.
11. Russell, Jesse and Ronald Cohn, eds. *Web Browser.* Print on Demand, 2013.
12. Stallings, William. *Computer Networking with Internet Protocols and Technology.* Delhi: Pearson, 2007.
13. Weinberg, Tamar. *The New Community Rules: Marketing on the Social Web.* Sebastopol, CA: O'Reilly, 2009.

INFORMATION LITERACY

Objective: To make the students aware of need, importance and concepts of information literacy both from users and library professionals point of view. Students are also exposed to learn different strategies and models need to be adopted for different types of libraries.

Unit 1: Emergence of Information Literacy

- Information Society and Information Literacy
- Information Literacy: Definition, Models and Standards
- Information Literacy: Strategic Plan
- Information Literacy and Lifelong Learning

Unit 2: ICT and Media Literacy

- Computer Literacy and E-Literacy
- Digital Literacy

- Media Literacy
- Information Literacy and Bridging the Digital Divide

Unit 3: Information Literacy and Libraries

- School, College and University Libraries
- Public Libraries
- Special Libraries
- Information Literacy and LIS Education

Unit 4: Policy and Advocacy

- Information Literacy: Initiatives and Forms in USA, UK and Australia
- Policies, Guidelines and Standards: UNESCO, IFLA and ALA
- Information Literacy: Skills and Competencies
- Information Literacy: Best Practices

Note: This course comprises 4 credits (4L+0T+0P) with internal marks (C1+C2) 40 and semester marks 60 (C3).

RECOMMENDED BOOKS

1. Association of College and Research Libraries. "Information Literacy Competency Standards for Higher Education-2000." ACRL, American Library Association. Accessed February 19, 2016. http://www.ala.org/acrl/standards/informationliteracycompetency.
2. Australian Library and Information Association. "Statement on Information Literacy for All Australians." ALIA. Accessed February 19, 2016. https://www.alia.org.au/about-alia/policies-standards-and-guidelines/statement-information-literacy-all-australians.
3. Bawden, David. "Information and Digital Literacies: A Review of Concepts." *Journal of Documentation* 57, No. 2 (2001): 218-59.

4. Bruce, Christine Susan. *The Seven Faces of Information Literacy*. Adelaide: Auslib Press, 1997.
5. Council of Australian University Librarians. *Information Literacy Standards*. Canberra: Council of Australian University Librarians, 2001.
6. Association of College and Research Libraries. Presidential Committee on Information Literacy, American Library Association. (1989). Final Report. Chicago: American Library Association. http://www.ala.org/ala/acrl/acrlpubs/whitepapers/presidential.htm.
7. Society of College, National and University Libraries. "Information Skills in Higher Education: A SCONUL Position Paper-1999." Society of College, National and University Libraries. 1999. Accessed February 19, 2016. http://www.sconul.ac.uk/activities/inf_lit/papers/Seven_pillars.html.
8. Torras, Maria-Carme and Tove Pemmer Sætre. *Information Literacy Education: A Process Approach: Professionalising the Pedagogical Role of Academic Libraries*. Oxford: Chandos Pub., 2009.

6

Open Elective (OE) Courses

E-RESOURCES

Objective: To make the students aware of different types of e-resources in different disciplines and their use for learning and research activities.

Unit 1: Types of e-Resources

- E-books, E-journals, E-reports, ETD
- Access to E-Resources through Library Consortia (UGC-INFONET Digital Library Consortium, INDEST-AICTE, National Knowledge Resource Consortium)
- Open Educational Resources

Unit 2: Web Resources

- Science and Technology
- Humanities
- Social Sciences
- Evaluation of Web Resources

Note: This course comprises 2 credits (2L+0T+0P) with internal marks (C1+C2) 40 and semester marks 60 (C3).

RECOMMENDED BOOKS

1. White, Andrew C. and Eric Djiva Kamal. *E-metrics for Library and Information Professionals: How to Use Data for Managing and Evaluating Electronic Resource*

Collections. London: Facet, 2006.

2. Rosa, Cathy De. *Perceptions of Libraries and Information Resources: A Report to the OCLC Membership*. Dublin, OH: OCLC Online Computer Library Center, 2005.
3. Rennie, Frank, and Tara Morrison. *E-Learning and Social Networking Handbook: Resources for Higher Education*. New York: Routledge, 2011.
4. Bobick, James E. and G. Lynn. Berard. *Science and Technology Resources: A Guide for Information Professionals and Researchers*. Library and Information Science Text Series. Santa Barbara, CA: Libraries Unlimited, 2011.
5. Wikoff, Karin. *Electronic Resources Management in the Academic Library: A Professional Guide*. Santa Barbara, CA: Libraries Unlimited, 2012.
6. Allen, Michael W. *Successful E-learning Interface: Making Learning Technology Polite, Effective, and Fun*. San Francisco, CA: Pfeiffer, 2011.
7. Breivik, Patricia Senn., E. Gordon Gee and Patricia Senn Breivik. *Higher Education in the Internet Age: Libraries Creating a Strategic Edge*. Westport, CT: Praeger Publishers, 2006.
8. Clayton, Peter and G.E. Gorman. *Managing Information Resources in Libraries: Collection Management in Theory and Practice*. London: Library Association Pub., 2001.
9. Clark, Ruth Colvin and Richard E. Mayer. *E-learning and the Science of Instruction: Proven Guidelines for Consumers and Designers of Multimedia Learning (ELearning and the Science of Instruction)*. Pfeiffer, 2011.
10. Siemens, Raymond George, and Susan Schreibman. *A Companion to Digital Literary Studies*. Malden, MA: Blackwell Pub., 2007.
11. Covey, Denise Troll. *Usage and Usability Assessment:*

Library Practices and Concerns. Washington, DC: Digital Library Federation, Council on Library and Information Resources, 2002.

COMMUNITY INFORMATION SERVICE

Objective: To acquaint students with need and purpose of community information services to make them learnt in developing community information center to cater the information needs of a specific community.

Unit 1: Basics of Community Information

- Community Information: Definition, Origin and Scope
- Need for and Sources of Community Information
- Role of Libraries in Dissemination of Community Information

Unit 2: Community Information Services

- Community Information Services: Meaning, Types and Target Users
- Community Information Centres: Planning and Role of Information Services
- Community Information Services to Specific Communities
  a) Rural, Urban and Metropolitan Communities
  b) Industrial, Business Communities
  c) Academic, Research, Institutional and R & D Communities
  d) Physically/Mentally Disadvantaged Communities
  e) Children, Women and Senior Citizens
- Community Information Services in India, UKand USA

Note: This course comprises 2 credits (2L+0T+0P) with internal marks (C1+C2) 40 and semester marks 60 (C3).

RECOMMENDED BOOKS

1. B. Ramesh Babu and S. Gopalakrishnan. *Information, Communication, Library, and Community Development*. Delhi: B.R. Publishing Corporation, 2004.
2. Bunch, Allan. *Community Information Services: Their Origin, Scope, and Development*. London: Bingley, 1982.
3. Rao, Chandrasekhara. *Library Services for Tribal Community*. Delhi: Delta Publishing House, 1996.
4. Childers, Thomas and Joyce A. Post. *The Information-poor in America*. Metuchen, NJ: Scarecrow Press, 1975.
5. Durrance, Joan C. *Armed for Action: Library Response to Citizen Information Needs*. New York, NY: Neal-Schuman Publishers, 1984.
6. Kahn, Alfred J. *Neighborhood Information Centers; a Study and Some Proposals*. New York: Columbia University School of Social Work, 1966.
7. Sarada, K. *Rural Library Services in India*. New Delhi: Ess Ess Publications, 1986.
8. Vashishth, C.P., ed. *Libraries as Rural Community Resource Centres: Papers & Proceedings of the Workshop on Rural Community Resource Centres, New Delhi, August 28-29, 1992*. Delhi: B.R. Publishing Corporation, 1995.
9. Voos, Henry. *Information Needs in Urban Areas; a Summary of Research in Methodology*. New Brunswick, NJ: Rutgers University Press, 1969.
10. Warner, Edward S., Ann D. Murray and Vernon E. Palmour. *Information Needs of Urban Residents*. Washington: US Bureau of Libraries and Learning Resources, 1973.

7

Advantages and Challenges

The global scenario of higher education has compelled a number of reforms in higher education in which UGC has initiated adoption of Choice Based Credit System (CBCS) in higher education institutions to ensure quality, excellence and efficiency. Besides, the increase in gross enrolment ratio in higher education institutions is also an alarming momentum to maintain quality in higher education falling in line with uniform practices and procedures compatible to international standards. The new system not only serves the purpose of credit based courses/programmes but the major emphasis is on mobility of students from one area to another area which is interdisciplinary in nature, transfer of credit within and outside of institution, examination evaluation and grading system. Since many higher education institutions (universities and colleges) have adopted CBCS at UG and PG level in the last 3-4 years, now these institutions are witnessing a number of advantages and challenges for its effective implementation, learning outcome and management of courses to assure quality and excellence.

Students Evaluation through Letter Grades and Grade Points

The UGC recommends a 10-point grading points system with the letter grades as mentioned in Table-1.The credits are converted into grades, Grade points and credit points. Based on this, calculations are made to derive Semester Grade Point Average (SGPA) and Cumulative Grade Point Average (CGPA).

Table 1: Letter Grades and Grade Points

Letter Grades		*Grade Points*
O	Outstanding	10
A^+	Excellent	9
A	Very good	8
B^+	Good	7
B	Above Average	6
C	Average	5
P	Pass	4
F	Fail	0
Ab.	Absent	0

Cumulative Grade Point Average (CGPA): It is a measure of overall cumulative performance of student over all semester. The CGPA is the ratio of total credit points secured by a student in various courses in all semesters and the sum of the total credits of all courses in all the semesters. It is expressed up to two decimal places.

Grade Point: It is a numerical weight allotted to each letter grade on a 10-point scale.

Letter Grade: It is an index of the performance of students in a said course. Grades are denoted by letters O, A+, A, B+, B, C, P and F.

Semester Grade Point Average: It is a measure of performance of work done in a semester. It is ratio of total credit points secured by a student in various courses registered in a semester and the total course credits taken during that semester. It shall be expressed up t two decimal places.

Transcript or Grade Card or Certificate: Based on the

grades earned, a grade certificate shall be issued to all the registered students after every semester. The grade certificate will display the course details (code, title, number of credits, grade secured) along with SGPA of that semester and CBPA earned till that semester.

The following are some of the advantages and challenges faced by universities and colleges.

Advantages of CBCS

1. Seamless Mobility

Mobility of students across departments/institutions and countries not only benefit the students in quest of knowledge in emerging areas but also facilitates potential employers to assess the performance of the students. It is also possible that a student can go to other university in India or abroad and study there and earn some credits for a semester period and come back to his parent university.

2. Inter-disciplinary Approach

CBCS aimed at student centric education and empowered students to become globally competitive. Further students opt for open electives and get an opportunity of interdisciplinary approach in learning and selecting the subjects of their own choice to develop specialization later.

3. Transfer of Credits

Transfer of credits is another unique feature of CBCS which allows transfer credit along with mobility students whether inter or intra University. The system allows a student in saving the time required for completion of a programme without going for second time admission from the beginning of the course in another institution. Credits earned during the former institution are transferred to later institution where the student is enrolled and same is in case of within a university system in which one student goes to another department for open elective course, at the end of the semester, the credit earned by the student is transferred to the parent department.

4. Continuous Performance Evaluation of Students

CBCS allows continuous assessment of learner through C1 and C2. In each stage there are three evaluation components (test/assignment/seminar/group discussion /tutorial/ presentation/etc) and in the whole process a student can make his/her self evaluation and learn at own pace.

5. Flexibility in Designing Curriculum

The CBCS pattern allows flexibility to design a particular course starting from 2 credit-6 credit depending on what type of course it is such as Foundation, Core, Soft/ specialized, Open Elective. Each type of course is unique in its contents and covers theoretical and practical aspects to enhance both knowledge and skills of a learner. Library and Information Science being a professional and practical based course, the curriculum is in built with both professional knowledge and skills.

6. International Recognition

The well defined semester system, types of courses, measuring each course in terms of credit, credit transfer, assessment and evaluation system, grading are some of the unique features of CBCS and well recognised internationally. Besides grading the performance of the students in line with international practice is another advantage of CBCS.

7. Students Autonomy

In the whole pattern of CBCS, utmost care is taken in granting students autonomy while selecting the courses on his/her own choice of courses, flexibility in assessment of internal tests in the form of tests, seminars and colloquiums, group discussion, assignments, repeating the papers in case of poor performance to make the system more learner centric.

Challenges

1. Problems in CBCS Implementation

Implementation of CBCS need a number of academic exercises such as, core committee to frame the guidelines for implementation based on UGC notification, availability of cluster class rooms, easy movement and transportation facilities for students from one Department to other Department, uniform semester routine indicating days and time allotted for OE classes, selection of OE by students according to their choice/preference, timely submission and return of marks of OE students to the parent Department are some of the problems which need to be resolved immediately by the CBCS core committee.

2. Infrastructure

Universities are continuously facing challenges with regard to inadequate physical, human and financial resources including ICT infrastructures. Cramped class rooms, inadequate faculties, problems of library and laboratory facilities need drastic improvements to support teaching, learning activities mandated by CBCS. Besides, large scale office automation, smart class rooms, MOOC, Wi-Fi facilities, digital library and e-resources, e-governance, digital evaluation, and digital printing of mark-sheets and certificates are some of the essential requirements for implementation of CBCS.

3. *Multiplicity of Authorities*

The universities are categorized into four categories namely, Central, State, Deemed and Private Universities. There are multiplicities with regard to governance and management. Therefore, uniform policies with regard to credit transfer for inter and intra universities need to be evolved to make the students' mobility more flexible.

4. *Support from Stakeholders*

The success of higher education system depends upon the close coordination among the state and central functionaries like university authority concerned like UGC, MHRD, AIU, AICTE, NAAC etc. A positive attitude from among all the authorities shall help the universities to overcome a number of constraints and challenges. Confrontation attitude by any single authority can march the whole spirit of reforms in higher education in general and CBCS in particular.

As a whole the introduction of CBCS in higher education institutions in India has brought systemic changes in emphasizing two key concepts—Choice and Assessment. Standardizing curriculum based on credits, uniform procedures and practices with regard to examination and assessment, grading pattern are some of the unique features to make it at par with international standards. This will pave the way for establishment of more foreign universities in India and offer more courses. Besides, students are expected to be more serious and sincere in studies in exhibiting their true performance level on a scientific scale. MHRD and UGC may constantly monitor the newly adopted dynamic system of higher education and address all issues arising out of this by providing full academic and financial support to make it more vibrant, cost effective and learner centric.

Abbreviations and Acronyms

AACR-IIR	Anglo-American Cataloguing Rules–IInd revised
AGRIS	International Information System for Agricultural Sciences and Technology
AICTE	All India Council for Technical Education
ALISE	Association for Library and Information Science Education
ASLIB/AIM	Association for Special Libraries and Information Bureaux (Old)/Association for Information Management (New)
BIS	Biodiversity Information System
BLIS	Bachelor in Library and Information Science
CAS	Current Awareness Service
CBCS	Choice Based Credit System
CC	Colon Classification
CCC	Classified Catalogue Code
CCF	Common Communication Format
CCTV	Closed-circuit Television
CDC	Curriculum Development Committee
CEP	Continuing Education Programme
CLIS	Certificate Course in Library and Information Science
CLS	Certificate in Library Science
COMPASS	Computer-Assisted Surveillance System/ Computer-Assisted Scheduling System

CPM	Critical Path Method
CSIR	Council of Scientific and Industrial Research
CSST	Curriculum Stipulated Study Tour
DDC	Dewey Decimal Classification
DDS	Document Delivery Service
DEC	Distance Education Council
DELNET	Developing Library Network (New), Delhi Library Network (Old)
DESIDOC	Defence Scientific Information and Documentation Centre
DLIS	Department of Library and Information Science
DLS	Diploma in Library Science
DOAJ	Directory of Open Access Journals
DOAR	Directory of Open Access Repositories
DRTC	Documentation Research and Training Centre
DSS	Decision Support System
ENVIS	Environmental Information System
ERNET	Education and Research Network
FRAD	Functional Requirements for Authorized Description
GARR	Guidelines for Authority Records and References
HTML	Hypertext Markup Language
IACR	Information Analysis Consolidation and Repackaging
IASLIC	Indian Association of Special Libraries and Information Centres
IATLIS	Indian Association of Teachers in Library and Information Science
ICSSR	Indian Council of Social Science Research
ICT	Information and Communication Technology
IFLA	International Federation of Library Associations and Institutions

IIT	Indian Institute of Technology
ILA	Indian Library Association
IME-ICC	IFLA Meeting of Experts on International Cataloguing Code
INDEST	Indian National Digital Library in Engineering Science and Technology
INFLIBNET	Information and Library Network
INIS	International Nuclear Information System
INSDOC	Indian National Scientific Documentation Centre
IPR	Intellectual Property Rights
IR	Information Retrieval
IR	Institutional Repository
ISAR	Information Storage and Retrieval
ISBD	International Standard Bibliographic Description
ISBN	International Standard Book Number
ISDN	Integrated Services Digital Network
ISO	International Organization for Standard
ISSN	International Standard Serial Number
KWAC	Key Word Augmented with Context
KWIC	Key Word In Context
KWOC	Key Word Out of Context
LCSH	Library of Congress Subject Heading
LIS	Library and Information Science
M.Phil	Master of Philosophy
MARC	Machine Readable Catalogue
MEDLARS	Medical Literature Analysis and Retrieval System
MIS	Management Information System
MLIS	Master in Library and Information Science
MS-DOS	Microsoft Disk Operating System
NASSDOC	National Social Science Documentation Centre

NASSDOC	National Social Science Documentation Centre
NCTE	National Council for Teachers Education
NICNET	National Information Centre Network
NISCAIR	National Institute for Science Communication and Information Resources
NKN	National Knowledge Network
N-LIST	National Library and Information Services Infrastructure for Scholarly Content
OAI	Open Access Initiatives
OAI-PMH	Open Archives Initiative-Protocol for Metadata Harvesting
OCLC	Online Computer Library Centre
OCR	Optical Character Recognition
OJS	Open Journal System
OPAC	Online Public Access Catalogue
OSI	Open Systems Interconnection
PDF	Portable Document Format
PERT	Program Evaluation and Review Technique
PGDIT	Post Graduate Diploma in Information Technology
PGDLAN	Post Graduate Diploma in Library Automation and Networking
Ph.D	Doctorate in Philosophy
PIS	Patent Information System
PKP	Public Knowledge Project
POPSI	Postulate Based Permuted Subject Indexing
POSDCORB	Planning, Organizing, Staffing, Directing, Coordinating, Reporting and Budgeting
PRECIS	Preserved Context Index System
RDA	Resource Description and Access
RFID	Radio Frequency Identification
ROAR	Registry of Open Access Repositories
RRRLF	Raja Rammohun Roy Library Foundation

RTI	Right to Information
SCI	Science Citation Index
SDI	Selective Dissemination of Information
SSCI	Social Science Citation Index
SWOT	Strength, Weaknesses, Opportunities and Threat (Old) The Association for Information Management (New)
UDC	Universal Decimal Classification
UGC	University Grants Commission
UNESCO	United Nations Educational, Scientific and Cultural Organization
UNIMARC	Universal Machine Readable Catalogue
XML	eXtensible Markup Language

Bibliography

1. Ahmad, Nasiruddin. "Library Education in Bangladesh Needs Modernization." *Journal of Library and Information Science* 13 (1988): 143.
2. Allan, Barbara. *E-learning and Teaching in Library and Information Services*. London: Facet Publishing, 2002.
3. Amerendra, Pani. *Globalization of Indian Higher Education*. New Delhi: Association of Indian Universities, 2003.
4. Amidon, Debra M. *Innovation Strategy for the Knowledge Economy*. Oxford: Butterworth, 2001.
5. Arora, Jagdish and K. Manoj Kumar. *Open Access, Open Source, Open Libraries (O³): Proceedings: November 6-7, 2008 at Nagaland University, Dimapur, Nagaland.*
6. Association of Indian Universities. *Handbook on Library & Information Science*. New Delhi: AIU, 2004.
7. Asundi, A.Y. "Specialization in Library and Information Science Education." *Herald of Library Science* 30 (1991): 249.
8. Babu, Ramesh B. "Students Opinion Survey on Library and Information Science Courses through Distance Education." *ILA Bulletin* 31 (1996): 84.
9. Barman, R.K. "Library Education in Assam: A Case Study of Gauhati School." *ILA Bulletin* 32 (1997): 34.
10. Bhargava, Surendra Singh. Gopal Das and Sonal Singh. *Trends in Library and Information Science: (Essays in Honour of Professor G.D. Bhargava)*. New Delhi: Gyan Pub., 2000.
11. Bhattacharyya, G. "On Teaching of Library and Information Science." *SRELS Journal of Information Management* 28, No. 2 (1991): 68-81.

12. Biniwal, J.C. and Karisiddapa. "The Role of Library in Learning." *Library Herald* 25 (1986): 1.
13. Boon, George S. "The State of Library Education in India." *Annals of Library and Documentation.* 15 (1968): 53-55.
14. Bowden, Russel. *Library Education Programmes in Developing Countries with Special Reference to Asia: Proceedings of the Unesco Pre-IFLA Conference Seminar on Library Education Programmes in Developing Countries with Special Reference to Asia, Quezon City, Manila, 15-19 Aug. 1980*. London: Library Association, 1982.
15. Carroll, Michael L. and W. Scott Downs. *Cyber Strategies: How to Build an Internet-based Information System.* New York: Van Nostrand Reinhold, 1996.
16. Cassidy, (Anita). *A Practical Guide to Information System Strategic Planning*. Boca Raton: St. Lucie Press, 1998.
17. Chahal, S.S. "Choice Based Credit System: Some Frequently Asked Questions." *University News* 54, No. 4 (2016): 3-9.
18. Chakravarty, N.C. "Education for Librarianship in Service and Correspondences Courses." *ILA Bulletin* 4 (1968): 75.
19. Chandraiah, I. "Library in Distance Education." *Herald of Library Science* 34 (1995): 14.
20. Chowdhury, G. G., Paul F. Burton, David McMenemy and Alan Poulter. *Librarianship: An Introduction*. London: Facet Publishing, 2008.
21. Devarjan, G. and K.A. Isaac. *New Challenges in Librarianship.* New Delhi: Ess Ess Publications, 2001.
22. Devi, K. Sugatri. "Curriculum in On-Campus and Off-Campus Library and Information Science Programmes in India—A Comparative Study." *ILA Bulletin* 32 (1997): 10.
23. Estabrook, Leigh and Montaque Rae-Anne. *Library and Information Science Education/Encyclopedia of Library and Information Science*. 2nd ed. Vol. 4.
24. Gayasuddin, D.K. Sharma and V. Mani. "Library and Information Science Education in the United States of America." *ILA Bulletin* 24 (1989): 37.
25. Gupta, Das. "Higher Education and National Development." *Library Herald* 11 (1969): 18-31.
26. Gupta, O.P. "LIS Training Curricula and National Approach." *Herald of Library Science* 41 (2002): 48.

27. Gupta, P.K. "Library and Information Science Curriculum Development." *Annals of Library Science and Documentation* 25 (1978): 3-21.
28. Harinaryana, N.S. and K.R. Nalini. "Changing Dimensions of Libraries and the Implications of Library Science Education in India." *Herald of Library Science* 33 (1994): 11.
29. India, Ministry of Information & Broadcasting. "PM's Remarks at the Launch of the Knowledge Commission." *Employment News*. August 13-19, 2005.
30. India. Task Force for India's Development as Knowledge Society. *India as Knowledge Superpower: Strategy for Transformation, Task Force Report*. New Delhi: Planning Commission, Government of India, 2001.
31. Kapoor, S.K. and S.N. Banerjee. "Education for Library and Information Science: Need for a Rational Approach." *IASLIC Bulletin* 31 (1986): 63-71.
32. Karandi, A.G. "Areas and Methods of Research in Library and Information Science." *IASLIC Bulletin* 34 (1989): 105.
33. Khandwala, Vidyut. "New Approach to Objectives of Library Education." *ILA Bulletin* 4 (1968): 73.
34. Khurshid, Anis. "Standards for Library Education in Burma, Ceylon, India and Pakistan." *Annals of Library Science and Documentation* 17 (1970): 23-24.
35. Khurshid, Anis. "Intellectual Foundations of Library Education." *Herald of Library Science* 7, No. 4 (1968): 225-39.
36. Kumar, Krishan and Jaideep Sharma. *Library and Information Science Education in India*. New Delhi: Har-Anand Publications, 2009.
37. Kumar, Krishan. "Framework for National Policy on Research and Education in Library and Information Science." *Library Herald* 22 (1983): 79.
38. Kumar, Krishan. "Library Education in India in the 1960's." *Library Herald* 13 (1971): 79-89.
39. Kumar, P.S.G. *Foundations of Library and Information Science: (Paper 1 of UGC Model Curriculum)*. Delhi: B.R. Pub., 2003.
40. Lazer, Peter. "Some Considerations on the Education and Training of Librarians and Information Specialists." *Annals of Library Science and Documentation* 31 (1984): 1-12.

41. *Libraries, Gateways to Knowledge: A Roadmap for Revitalization.* New Delhi: National Knowledge Commission, 2007.
42. Library Association. *Professional Education and Training for Library and Information Work: A Review.* London: Library Association on Behalf of the Council, 1986.
43. Madegowda, J. "University Grants Commission Guidelines on Choice Based Credit System: Some Observations and Inputs." *University News* 53, No. 18 (2015): 3-10.
44. Mangla, P.B., D.R. Kalia, Neela Jagannathan and M.K. Jain. *Library and Information Services in India: States and Union Territories: On the Eve of New Millennium.* Delhi: Shipra Publications, 2001.
45. Marshall, D.N. "Education for Librarianship in India." *ILA Bulletin* 4 (1968): 53.
46. Martyn, John, Peter Vickers and M. Feeney. *Information UK 2000.* London: Bowker-Saur, 1990.
47. Mathan, Inder Vir, and Urmil Gupta. "Need for Rethinking on Library and Information Science Education in India." *ILA Bulletin* 24 (1989): 208.
48. Meadows, Jack. "Educating the Information Professional." In *Perspectives in Information Management*, edited by Charles Oppenhiem. Vol. 1. London: Butterworth, 1989.
49. Morrell, Deel and Gamlen. *Electronic Networks: Potential Liabilities for Network Provides and Users Organization.* London: McGraw Hill, 1995.
50. Mukherjee, A.K. "Reference Sources and Services in Education." *Library Herald* 12 (1970): 178-90.
51. NAAC. *Guidelines on Quality Indicators in Library and Information Services: Affiliated/Constituent Colleges*. Bangalore: NAAC, 2005.
52. Nanda, V.K. "Library Oriented Education." *ILA Bulletin* 8 (1972): 103.
53. Nelamaeghan, A. "User Orientation' in Library and Information Studies Curriculum: Some Aspects with Special Reference to Developing Countries." *Journal of Library and Information Science* 10 (1985): 53.
55. Pitroda, Sam. *Report to the Nation, 2006.* New Delhi: National Knowledge Commission, Government of India, 2007.
55. Prasher, R.G. *LIS: Parameters and Perspectives.* Vol. 1. New Delhi:

Concept, 1997.

56. Raghavan, K.S. *Library and Information Science Education.* Vol. 2. New Delhi: Ess Ess, 1998
57. Raghvan, Hema. "SWOT Analysis of CBCS." *University News* 53, no. 27 (2015): 9-11. 2015.
58. Rahaman, P.F. and I. Ramabrahmam. "Promoting Excellence in Higher Education: Is Choice Based Credit System a Feasible Approach?" *University News* 53, No. 20 (2015): 250-53.
59. Rajaram, Shyama. "Library Education in Gujarat." *Library Herald* 35 (1998): 79.
60. Raju, Narasimha. "Distance Education and Libraries." *Library Herald* 37 (2000): 258.
61. Rao, B.V.R. and K.S. Deshpande. "Stray Comments on Library Education." *ILA Bulletin* 4 (1968): 56.
62. Rath, Pravakar and Linda Smith. "Web-Based/Virtual Mode of Library and Information Science Education in US: Opportunities and Challenges." *Proceedings of International Conference on Information Management in a Knowledge Society: 21-25 February 2005: Conference Papers.* Vol. 1. New Delhi: Allied Publishers Pvt. Ltd., 2005.
63. Rath, Pravakar. "Collection Development in Electronic Environment and Role of Library and Information Professionals." *Asia Library News*, March 2002.
64. Rath, Pravakar. "Education and Training of Information Professionals in Indian University Libraries." In *Information Technology Applications in Academic Libraries(CALIBER-1997).* Proceedings. Ahmedabad: INFLIBNET, 1997.
65. Rath, Pravakar. "Education for Information: Emerging Scope and Challenges in India." *Annals of Library and Information Studies* 49, No. 3 (2002): 99-106.
66. Rath, Pravakar. "Human Resource Development Through Distance Mode Library and Information Science Education in India." *Asia Library News* 6, No. 1 (2003).
67. Rath, Pravakar. "National Mission on Libraries (A Step towards Strengthening the Library System in the Country)." *AIU - News* 51, No. 1 (2013).
68. Rath, Pravakar. "Preparing Library and Information Professionals for 21st Century: Issues and Challenges for LIS

Educators in India." Proceedings of International Conference Volume on the Occasion of Asia-Pacific Conference on Library and Information Education and Practice Preparing Information Professionals for Leadership in the New Age, Nanyang Technological University, Singapore. 2006.

69. Rath, Pravakar. "Professional Competency Building Through Distance Mode Library and Information Science Programmes with Special Reference to MLIS Programme of Indira Gandhi National Open University (IGNOU): A Case Study." *Library Herald*, March 2005.
70. Rewadikar, Shalini. "Continuing Education for Teachers of Library and Information Science." *ILA Bulletin* 15 (1979): 38.
71. Sen Gupta, Benoyendra. "Library Education in India: Let Us Look Hard at It." *ILA Bulletin* 4 (1968): 73.
72. Seth, M.K. and D.B. Ramesh. "Library Education through Open University System: Challenges for Library Professionals in India." *ILA Bulletin* 32 (1997): 5.
73. Sharma, J.B. *Elements of Library Science*. New Delhi: Kanishka Publishers, 1996.
74. Sharma, Jaideep. "Professional Competencies, Employer Expectation and Curriculum for LIS Education in India." *ILA Bulletin* 38 (2000): 181.
75. Shuman, Bruce A. *Issues for Libraries and Information Science in the Internet Age*. Englewood, CO: Libraries Unlimited, 2001.
76. Singh, Jagtar. "Globalization of Library and Information Science Education via the Internet." *Library Herald* 39 (2001): 71.
77. Skriphina, T.I. and G.G. Firsov. "The System in Library Education in the USSR." *Annals of Library Science and Documentation* 15 (1968): 103-11.
78. Swaminathan, M.S. "Mission 2007: Every Village a Knowledge Centre." *The Hindu*, November 25, 2005.
79. Umapathy, Setty K. "Non-formal Education: Educational Goals and their Implications to Library Service." *Annals of Library Science and Documentation* 20 (1973): 69-74.
80. University Grants Commission. *UGC Model Curriculum: Library and Information Science*. New Delhi: UGC, 2002.
81. University Grants Commission. "University and Society." In *Proceedings of the Conference of Vice-Chancellors of the Central and*

State Universities. New Delhi: UGC, 2011.

82. University Grants Commission. *Inclusive and Qualitative Expansion of Higher Education: Compilation Based on the Deliberations of the Working Group for Higher Education in the 12th Five-Year Plan (2012-17)*. New Delhi: UGC, 2011.
83. University Grants Commission. *UGC Draft Regulation on Minimum Qualifications for Appointment of Teachers and Other Academic Staff in Universities and Colleges and Measures for the Maintenance of Standards in Higher Education 2010*. New Delhi: UGC, 2010.
84. Verma, S.C. "New Education Policy and Libraries." *ILA Bulletin* 21 (1986): 100.
85. Vijaya Kumari, J. "Changing Scenario in Library and Information Science Education in India: Some Observations." *Herald of Library Science* 40 (2001): 186.
86. Yusuf, Mohammad. "Survey of LIS Schools in India in Relation to Geographical Distribution." *IASLIC Bulletin* 40 (1995): 169.